# THE MANLY MARRIAGE MANUAL

*Fifty Ways to Man Up to Your Wife*

*Rob Gleghorn*

*For Heidi*

*If it weren't for you, I wouldn't be married. If it weren't for you, I wouldn't have a life of any real earthly value or a reason to write anything in the first place. Because of you and all the mistakes I've made over the years, this book has real merit in showing others what not to do in their relationships. Thank you for being the best part of our one flesh…and for providing the endless war stories that follow. I love you more than you know.*

# INTRODUCTION

Marriages are like rock bands…I'm amazed they stay together. Let me start off with the fact that I don't like introductions. I'm not even sure why a preface exists other than as space to write something before I start writing something. I will say this as an intro, however, even though I'm not the one who coined it, and I don't know who did: "Love is blind, but marriage is a real eye-opener." So true. Don't get me wrong—if I could do it all over again, I would marry the same beautiful lady. The difference is that I would start doing the things that really matter much, much earlier in the marriage. I used to think that the four pillars to a man's heart were food, sex, sleep, and television. (I'm not that far off, actually.) This is a manual focused on your woman, however.

And this manual is written by a man, for a man. I realize a woman may somehow magically find this book to "help" her husband or boyfriend, and chances are, men, that your woman showed this to you after a full day of browsing Facebook and Pinterest. That's fine; I hope every woman in North America buys sixty-two copies for every man she knows. But I want you ladies to know that you are not my target audience—the dudes are. Only men know how men think. And although we love the way you women look and smell, we really only understand each other.

For example, you men will notice that each blurb to follow is short, choppy, to the point, and filled with some serious humor to boot. (Trust me, I'm funny; just ask me.) This is because you will most likely be on the toilet while reading this, and you need a good starting and stopping point at all times...because you will be interrupted.

So it's 0130—that means "real early" for you men who never served in the US Armed Forces. (I just retired a couple years ago after doing twenty years of it...on purpose.) Anyhow, I couldn't sleep, so I decided to get up and write a book real quick in my spare time. I do some of my best thinking when I'm sleepy, slobbering on one end of my pillow—much like when I used to be in the military—so no telling what's coming in the chapters ahead.

The way I see it, books (and any form of teaching or learning for that matter) should meet two criteria. One, they should make me laugh. I read enough junk all day at my job and now in the headlines, none of which is usually funny (except for when the celebs do stupid things in an obvious "no stupid" zone). Even the comic strips today are kind of sucky, with the exception of *The Far Side*, which I can no longer find. I want to laugh. I need to laugh. You need to laugh. It's good for the soul, even if you can't remember why you thought it was funny ten minutes later.

The second item that has to be present in books (and people for that matter) is that they should have a freaking point. Why just read or listen to someone flapping their lips? So I (and you) need to have a point in the sense that what is written or spoken has an actual bearing on the lives of others. In other words, it should be truthful and therefore somehow make a difference in my life, not just in my thinking, but in how I live. If what you are saying or writing doesn't change my life for the better in some fashion, why are you wasting my time? (By the way, every boss in America needs to read that last line about 136 more times, especially the uniformed ones.) My goal is not to waste your time here either (any more than I already have).

So what could I possibly write about that is going to make a difference in your life? Let's go with marriage. Ah, that wonderful bliss you entered into so innocently, scared like a little lamb (or forced by a future father-in-law-UFC-type man), not knowing you were going to the slaughterhouse because you had no clue what you were getting yourself into. After twenty-eight years of marriage, I'm still not sure what I got myself into. I am plugging along like the rest of you. (OK, some of you newlyweds are zipping along having sex every single day, and the rest of you are wondering what series of decisions led you to where you are right now.) I have learned a few things along the way, however, and I will share some of my nuggets of wisdom with you…and not just a few things. My original intention was to write something lame along the lines of "101 Things a Husband Can Do to Make His Marriage Better." Once I started the list, however, I found myself being too hypocritical because I was struggling to do them all myself, so I landed at an even fifty for now. There are thousands more, but the heavy hitters are now in the palm of your hand.

And why would I list them? Because we men are simple creatures. I didn't say stupid, I said simple. We just want our tools in the same spot every time we go to the garage—simple. Try not to spend more than you make—what an easy concept. Turn off the flipping lights when you leave a room so I don't keep getting $650 electric bills. So easy to get. We like things laid out and orderly. Don't give me a bunch of psychobabble nonsense—just tell me what I need to do to make my life better. This manual is not just a how-to or touchy-feely manual, it's a what-the-heck-do-I-do-with-her manual. It is a simple to-do list, because if you're like me, I just want to know what I can do to make my woman happier. I will give you scores of things you can actually do to make your marriage better—time-tested things that work all the time, regardless of the emotional chaos your wife may be experiencing with or without waving a knife around at you.

So, gentlemen (and ladies who ignored what I said about this being a manual for men), there's my intro. My job is to entertain you and to make a difference in your lives via the written word. If I can do that, my time, sleepless nights, and energy have been worth it. I have cleverly titled each issue so you can easily find your way back to where you left off, so sit back and enjoy the ride (even if it's a porcelain one). If you are like me, you won't remember where you left off, so you'll end up reading several paragraphs more than once. No big deal. You need to hear it several times anyhow.

# WEAR NICE CLOTHES

If you are like me, this is not a *will* problem as much as it is a *skill* problem. It is the blind leading the blind. It is having the construction worker do your detailed neurosurgery; he has a good heart, wants the job, and truly desires to be helpful, he's just not qualified. What I mean is that I am willing to do it; I just lack the expertise to pick out a suitable outfit (for me or the children). Let me rephrase. I am more than content with what I pick out, and I find it plenty suitable—be it the half-cropped netlike jersey from 1981 or my parachute pants with twelve zippers or the same shirt I wore the last six times we went to church. It is she who is not content. So if I want to love *her*, the solution is to have her pick out my clothes and the kids' clothes ahead of time.

My wife is more than willing if I give her the option for a preemptive strike. This has helped alleviate mass fights after I am already dressed. I can't tell you how many times she has asked me to change shirts or pants or (my worst nightmare) shoes and underwear after I am already dressed. So now I give her a window of opportunity (like a clandestine Tibetan CIA operation) where she has about one minute and thirty seconds to find proper clothes for me and the kids to wear. (Here's a note for women: men don't wear outfits; we wear pants and a shirt that does or doesn't have to match. In our minds it's about speed—we wear whatever's on top of the drawer. So don't ask us what we prefer; just leave it on the bed and it will be exactly what we wanted... trust me.)

If all else fails, there's a 90 percent chance we'll pick out the blue shirt with the khaki pants again. Men, you have to initiate this one. Every weekend I remind my wife that she has to pick out what she likes or the sweats are coming out. Your piece is to ask her (nicely) to grab whatever it is she would like you to wear. In the rare circumstance you're one of those guys who dresses nicely all by yourself, good for you. You get to be one of the lucky ones who I don't have anything to say to this time, but trust me, your turn is coming.

# HER CUP FIRST

I know you probably don't even acknowledge you're alive until you're on coffee cup number two or three. I sometimes suck the grounds straight through a Krazy Straw for that early-morning jolt. But here's an opportunity to put her first and it costs you nothing (money-wise). If she is a tea person (I'll pray for you because apparently there are seven steps involved in making proper tea), get that kettle boiling right away when you get up, and bring the beverage to her while yours is still brewing or sitting there waiting.

If you're like me, I actually go to bed at night just thinking about how good "my precious" is going to be the next day. My coffee love is like an Old Testament concubine I keep on the side, but you and I cannot let her take first place in our lives. Your coffee concubine has to be the lesser treasure in your life each day. You may think this is a joke, but I have friends who spend more on Starbucks supplies than on their wives. If she doesn't like tea or coffee (she obviously isn't from the Northwest), get her juice or water (gag me). Either way, serve her cup first—you'll get more brownie points for doing this one thing than almost anything you do the rest of the day.

# DO THE EGGS

This one is simple. I have no problem doing this (especially on the weekends or days like today when it is snowing sideways and I still get paid for *not* being at work). During the week, it's just cereal for me and the kids anyhow, but come Saturday I start slapping bacon, eggs, toast, or wannabe McMuffins together like nobody's business. This is *my* kind of breakfast though. It's something funky from my childhood I suppose, but then again my father grew up in Arkansas, so biscuits and gravy are also considered normal to me. I've already warped my son, since he now considers my fine dish a delicacy—my daughter, not so much. Back to the wife.

The hard part comes in when my wife wants something healthy, which is almost every meal. For most men, breakfast has never been about health. I had to learn to spell, sound out, and concoct smoothies a few years ago. I'm talking about real smoothies too, not the kind my buddy makes in Washington with chocolate chips and ice. (Don't worry, Scott, no one will ever figure out who you are…most likely.) It wasn't until the last few years that I learned to make her a truly healthy shake: bark chips, lawn-mower shavings, lecithin, brewer's yeast, bananas, strawberries, grass grown indoors on a shelf, twelve ingredients that keep you regular, and a few things off the carpet. (I know, we men have no issues keeping ourselves regular 99 percent of the time, but our wives do. God just chose to give them more plumbing issues for some reason.)

Take this morning as a prime example on how to keep the spice in your marriage. I threw the eggs and cheese together all by myself! If you have a wife like mine, however, your roles are reversed in one or two areas. She likes foods that make my lips curl due to the hotness factor, so I threw some green chilies on my masterpiece and she loved it. (I can't eat the hot stuff any longer because it causes the "ring of fire" later, and I don't mean the kind between the continental plates.) The secret is to make breakfast taste good *and* be healthy; anyone can make food healthy, but to actually be willing to put it in your mouth takes real talent.

# CRANK THE FAN

O K, you're probably reading this right where I would read it—on the toilet. (Please see the previous "ring of fire" paragraph for clarity.) The question is whether you are doing your manly business while doing your "manly business." My wife constantly comes into the bathroom, flicks on the fan, sprays a variety of citrus fumes all over me, the floor, the walls, and sometimes even the tub, and then walks back out without saying a word. After twenty-seven years of marriage, I finally get it—she doesn't like stink... I'm guessing. So, men, let me help you with my newfound discovery.

Women don't care to smell men's intestinal tracts (even their own husband's) and understandably so. If you were to ever give me a written test as to whether this was true or false, I could get the right answer every time. In practice, however, I rarely turn on the fan. I certainly don't shut the door because I'm practicing situational awareness or I don't think about it or I just forget…or maybe in some sick way, I'm proud of my manly aroma.

My father used to say one could tell who the real man of the house was based on his ability to clear 2,500 square feet of living space in two minutes or less. (I now realize he just needed serious colon cleansing and was probably in his forties as well. No, Dad, not something to be proud of…this is something others are usually hospitalized for.) Any which way I rationalize it, none of my thinking makes my wife feel loved by me, so now I go out of my way to "cover my tracks" in any way I can. When I'm really on top of it, I even light these six-pound lilac candles that I paid way more for than I'm sure they're worth. Best fifty-two dollars I ever spent.

# YOUR WET TOWEL

I failed epically at this again not too long ago. I'm not sure where this one flaw of mine stems from or why we men consistently do it. (Maybe it's tied to toilet paper being put back on the roller.) For some magical reason, the towel just refuses to make it all the way back to the rack. It must be a good fifteen feet. I can't even retrace my steps to figure it out. I think I have a minor stroke between the shower and the bedroom because I have no memories of this time-travel portal. I have the towel on right after a shower, and I know I'll need it again just after I shave, but how it ends up on the bed is always a total mystery. It would make sense if I were doing a striptease for my wife to our standard jungle music (not that this has ever worked, but I try it at least weekly), but I think my wits get foggy somewhere in the chaos of the morning rush. I keep telling her I'm not doing it on purpose, and between you and me, I'm really not.

But, for the five hundredth time, I did it again. I don't know about your woman, but my wife is excellent at word pictures to "help" me figure out her emotional pain. She first used to tell me, "How would you like it if I left my underwear hanging around the house?" Now, any normal man would dare his wife to do such a thing. (This, of course, has the opposite effect, as this would actually be a preference of mine.) So she went to word picture number two. Lately, she has said, "How would you like it if I left a pile of my junk in the middle of the garage every day?" Now I get it. That would be an automatic no go in our relationship. Would Jesus have allowed a cluttered carpentry shop? No! This would irritate the living snot out of me. Then I tell her that's not even something to joke about. She's tried to convince me over the years that my wet towel feels the same (which can't be possible), but at least I know where she's coming from.

Oh, and leaving it on the floor (I found out) is just as bad—it has to make it back to where it belongs and be folded correctly on the little silver bar. If you don't believe this last little nugget of truth, imagine she uses your extension cords every day, but instead of rolling them into nice tidy bundles (the way they were found), she gathers them in several knots and throws them across the garage floor and can't remember how they got there. Fair enough—I can do a little towel folding for her, but I'm going to have to bungee that little towel to get it all the way back on the rack. Now there's an invention…a towel that snaps back, use after use. No extra effort required.

# DATE HER OFTEN

For some of you, this will equate to the hot-dog stand in front of Home Depot; that's fine, just make sure you bring her with you *and* talk to her. Sometimes we get so accustomed to not going anywhere due to work schedules and watching the kids that we forget to romance the one we love. And trust me…she wants to be romanced. (Her dream life hasn't come to fruition like she planned either!)

My wife tells me every Friday when I come home and kick my heels up that she is still "at the office." I'm ready to go into a coma, and she wants to go out. Your wife anticipated being swept off her feet by a knight in shining armor…and married you instead. Although I don't own a horse, I can at least take her downtown. (If your downtown is like mine, it has one Safeway and one Wal-Mart, so I really have to pull a serious "Cowboy Take Me Away" like the song says.)

Often, my wife and I will just go out for dessert or coffee, so the date doesn't have to be expensive. Your wife merely wants time alone with her lover (hopefully this is still you), so give it to her. You need to do this at least weekly. My wife and I have chosen Tuesdays as our date night, because Monday is typically a suckfest. Wednesday is our marriage study night (and my wife doesn't consider this a romantic date for some reason). Thursday is my manly men's group, which I'm convincing her makes me a better husband and father.

The point is to get out there and do something that allows "tune" time. (This is when we really tune into each other's hearts.) We even switch who does the planning from week to week so as to be more creative and allow the other person to tap into the soul. You have to be open to this one, however, because you will be getting some serious culture nights. Oh, and let me warn you ahead of time...not every date is awesome. Sometimes we talk about dumb stuff, like how the workday went or how bad my gas was that day. Other times, when we are more on target, we talk about each other and how much we appreciate one another. After all, who doesn't like a little love-on-me time now and then?

# WASH HER CAR

I know how you feel already. In fact, if you are still reading this manual, good for you. I used to have an immaculate four-wheel-drive pickup truck before I got married. I think it was because I had nothing but time on my hands. I was single, in the military, and had no bills back then. My whole paycheck went into my "chick magnet," so naturally I kept it spotless, since my only responsibility was to put gas in it.

Fast-forward twenty-seven years and two kids later. We now have a Dodge Durango—part manly vehicle, part min-ivan. To complete my man-van image, I put a brush guard on it and a ski rack (which has never been used, by the way). I have put dead deer in the back, however, so it has been stained with manly provider-ness over the years. In fact, I took the man-van out deer hunting a few years ago. All was good until I loaded the deer in the back. (Yes, it was at least a one hundred-pounder!) I even threw a tarp down to help keep the vehicle clean. The next day on our way to church, everyone was itching and scratching. The deer carcass had left us with about three million fleas. To make it worse, the dog had been in the car, so now fleas were in the house too. Hundreds of dollars, four flea bombs, and a couple thorough shampoos later, and everything was back to normal. I figure pound for pound the deer cost me about six hundred dollars more than going to Safeway. It was almost worth it (but mostly not).

So back to the car-cleaning issue. Between my wife and kids, our Dodge has enough food under the seats to feed a small camp of POWs. The glove box has so much junk in it, three pounds of crap fling to the floor every time you open it (which is why I never do). And still my wife wants me to clean it. I actually don't mind cleaning the car; I mind it getting filthy forty-five seconds later. This is especially true when she and the kids go to the beach the following day and build sand castles in the carpet with their feet. Then they stop for lunch and the kids have a cracker-stomping contest on the way home. Drives me insane.

At this writing, I can't say that keeping the car clean is one of my strong points. In fact, it would be a boldface lie to say I keep it clean. All I can say is that I know it's important to her and that it's on my radar to do it more often. Some of you are better at this one than some of the other things I have mentioned though. So if you're more like me, here's the fix: I used to be one of those guys who would never pay someone else to wash my vehicles. Today I have found that it's worth every dime. I don't have to get mad at the whole family for being filthy pigs, and she gets to enjoy a clean car. The key is to find a place (or a young person) who will do it for a decent price. There's no way I'm going to pay seventy-five dollars for a vacuum and quick wipe down, and my son is still a little too young to do it right...but the day is coming soon enough when he and his sister will be picking gummy bears out of the seat cracks with a toothpick and learning how Armor All makes tires glisten. So make her happy—clean it yourself at least once a month (or biweekly if your family is like mine), or be ready to pay the piper.

# QUICK TO LISTEN

R eally listen to her. Many times my wife will just start talking to me before I am locked on to the signal, and she'll ask that all-important question all men love: "Are you listening to me?" If you were to pan into my skull at that moment, you would see a clown going in circles on a unicycle, so the answer is always obvious: "No, I'm not." She always thinks this is strange, as if the autolistening feature should be in the "on" position at all times. For years now I have been trying to tell her the audio mechanism stays in the "off" mode to preserve energy, and sometimes the batteries aren't even installed...especially right after work when most of my mind juices have been used up by people I don't even like.

I will never forget the empty fruit bowl we used to have on our countertop. That's right—the key word here is *empty*. I used to come home and put my keys and wallet in it so I would always know where they were when it was time to run back out the door. One day she asked me not to put my wallet and keys in it any more. Sounded dumb to me because it wasn't being used anyhow. A few days later as I was doing paperwork, I started to put bills and other things in the fruit bowl to be mailed. Again my wife said not to put any bills in it or any of my stuff. There was still no fruit in the thing.

A few more days went by, and I found myself in rare form cleaning the kitchen. I started making a little pile of her things, and with nowhere to put them, I placed them in the fruit bowl so she could sift through them when she had a chance. Then I went to work. When I came home, steam and fire were billowing from her nostrils as she proceeded to tell me I didn't respect her and was the most insensitive man on the planet. For the life of me I couldn't figure out why she was even mad...until she pointed at the fruit bowl. I thought to myself, "I hadn't put my wallet or keys in it. I hadn't put any bills in it. All I did was stick some of *her* stuff in the bowl, so what was her problem?"

She then told me how obvious it was that she wanted nothing in the fruit bowl but fruit and that I had blatantly "crapped on her feelings," as she liked to say back then. Now any guy reading this knows this was not the case. Any woman reading this probably agrees with my wife, hence the topic title. So the next time your wife requests something from you, all I can say is ask more questions. Get clarity somehow because most of the time, "It ain't what you think it means, Cletus." And that's OK by itself. Loving your wife is about listening to her and trying to really find out what she needs, not necessarily just the words coming out of her lips.

# ALWAYS BE FESTIVE

So my little girl turned four years old on the Wednesday before I wrote this. What did I do? I jumped up that morning, got the kids dressed (all by myself), went and picked up her birthday cake, and still made it to church on time. Then I went to our favorite Mexican restaurant and ordered forty dollars' worth of quesadillas (not what I had planned, but that's how it turned out). Then I went to the Dollar Store to find the only pink plastic tablecloth in the whole city. By the way, if you ever have to buy decorations for any occasion, go to your nearest Dollar Store. They have all the junk you need, you don't have to shop long, and the prices are doable without becoming extra bitter. (I forget about this little hidden treasure every year for some reason.)

I epically failed to get forks, however, and had to run to another store four minutes after I returned. Supposedly, doing a small party at the local pool was going to save me money...not even close. I made twenty-three trips, spent about two hundred dollars more than I planned, and then spent forty-five minutes videotaping and snapping pictures of kids I didn't even know, all of whom were stuffing their fat little faces with my platter-o-quesadillas. Oh, did I mention it is now common courtesy to buy all the kids who attend your kid's birthday party their own presents as well? Whoever thought of this nice, loving gesture should be slapped for being the neighborhood fun dad and setting the precedent for the rest of us. Basically, the planning, preparation, and decorating kind of sucked, I have to admit, but it was worth it for my baby girl and my wife. So what's the moral of the story? I'm glad you asked.

You can and should be festive all the time—and not just at birthdays. You "get to" help be festive at Christmas, New Year's, Valentine's Day, St. Patrick's Day, Sweetest Day, and leap years if you're as lucky as me. That's what she really wants anyhow—not just your participation, but you *wanting* to celebrate with her and the kids.

This last Christmas was the second time in my life I put Christmas lights on the outside of the house, and now I remember why I had only done it twice. I had to climb on the icy roof by doing a half gainer triple twist off the top of the ladder. Then, instead of staying perfectly safe in the middle of the roof, I had to lean over the edge, Christmas lights in one hand, staple gun in the other. With wind blowing at 40 mph, the lights were finally up...and then I got to look for the short for an extra three hours.

After a minor repair, voilà! "Christmas Vacation" was in full swing with six hundred candle watts of pure power outlining the frame of our humble home. I was so proud. Three minutes went by in my mind, but it was soon February…and then the HOA sent me a nasty gram telling me to quit being such a redneck and to remove my Christmas creation. So I lovingly went outside and gave the little string a tug, thinking the staples would easily give way. The string ripped in half. So I tugged eleven more times…and put all twelve pieces in the trash. Mission accomplished, and only thirty bucks down the drain.

So if you think celebrating isn't that important, I dare you to ask your wife if she ever wants help with it. A friend of mine's wife actually left him, took the kids, and moved to Europe one year after he wouldn't help her wrap gifts, so don't underestimate this one. Being festive all the time is important to her. Don't even try to figure it out, just go with it. Just be prepared to spend a little money, and do it for every single occasion that comes up (regardless of how dumb you think the occasion is).

# FOLD SOME LAUNDRY

S orry to keep giving you extra gas with my titles. Remember that game you used to play with your buddies when you were younger when you tried to think of the most painful thing a man could endure? I believe my friends and I settled on the idea where a dude was supposed to slide down a huge razor blade into a pool of rubbing alcohol. Folding laundry is sort of like that for men.

Every time my wife leaves town, I pretty much live out of the washer and dryer—there is no folding. (It's like making the bed—you know it just gets messy again, so why bother?) I grab what I need from the dryer and it goes right back into the washing machine, maybe after four or five good hikes in it. I loathe folding laundry. I believe hell will involve laundry in some capacity. I know I'm supposed to be thankful for having clothes, and I am, but I would rather run around the house stark naked than have to fold one whole sock.

When my wife asks for my help in this area, I immediately see the razor blade and alcohol. I think to myself, "There has to be a fire somewhere that has the lives of small children at risk. There has to be some *Braveheart* task more in need of my services right now. Maybe a small war near the Pueblo Reservoir where I can get into a firefight and have to kick in doors."

If you find this as miserable as me, there's only one thing you can do to take away the sting—find the biggest, baddest, action-packed movie you can to watch (like *Rambo 8*), and you'll be able to tolerate the folding, get serious brownie points at the same time, and not know you're even doing it.

By the way, I did manage to get out of the whole washing-laundry phenomenon on the front end of our marriage. It's relatively simple: mix the darkest reds and the whitest whites together with the hottest water cycle just once, and she'll never "let" you wash the laundry again. Folding is tougher to get out of, however, and since this is a manual about doing great things for your wife, this is one thing we can do that's relatively easy (as long as we are preoccupied by some kind of blood and pillaging).

# GO TO WORK

T o most of us, this is a no-brainer, and really this sage-
like piece of advice is twofold. One, you need to get off
your butt and physically go earn a decent paycheck if you
aren't already. If it isn't decent and you find yourself buying
crates of Top Ramen at Costco to survive, you may need
two jobs until you get on your feet. I know some men who
are more like Cousin Eddie from the *Vacation* films, who
tend to "hold out for a management position." Stop jack-
ing around and get to work. Even if it's delivering pizzas,
get it done (as Dave Ramsey always says). There's no getting
around this unless you have a physical or mental problem
that prevents it. Men are obligated to provide for their families (even if it's just you and your wife). I had a friend once
who was married with seven kids. He wasn't working at all
and proceeded to tell me how he was going to start a fly-
fishing business. All he needed was a $40,000 loan to get

it started. I told him he was smoking crack, to go get a job, and to pursue this extra dream at night and on the weekends. (By the way, he never got any kind of job and he's no longer married.)

Some of you are thinking you need two incomes to survive. No, you don't. You need to quit spending more than you make. If you're poor, live like you're poor. My wife has always worked in some capacity, so don't get me wrong. She *can* work, but she shouldn't *have* to work. That's my job. That's your job. Today, my wife works from home, which was always my dream for her anyhow. Between two kids, school, a cat (don't get me started on why cats are going to hell), a turtle, a dog, a chinchilla, eighty-three self-inflicted activities, and keeping the house running smoothly, she doesn't have time for much else. But it's my job to work for her and the kids so they can function and get through life and school with a loving family and a solid roof over their heads. It even says in Proverbs 12:11 that "he who works his land will have abundant food, but he who chases fantasies lacks judgment." Trying to figure out what you are supposed to do as far as a calling is a good thing that you need to pursue, but you should always work your land and keep food on the table in the meantime. (By the way, if you haven't read *Quitter* by Jon Acuff, you're missing a real treat on closing the gap between your day job and your dream job. His book is 100 percent true and sarcastic...my two favorite elements in a book.)

Secondly, it's my job to work for her at home. She works for me every day in thousands of ways. In fact, everything I write about is about working for her. (Don't worry, a manual just for women will also someday hit the shelves, and we'll be able to sit back and say, "I told you it wasn't just me.") Some of you come home from work and plop on the couch after a hard day at work. Even I take a few minutes of downtime. (My wife will say it's more than a few minutes, but this is my manual.) But you can't live in the recliner every night. If you are one of those guys who have made it to level ten on *Halo* or have seen every episode of the *Twilight* movies—all right after work—you have issues. (Actually, if you are watching the *Twilight* movies, put this manual down immediately...this is for men.)

Life isn't about video games and television, my brothers, especially if there's work to be done around the house, and trust me, there always is. I know we sometimes need to come home and kill a few zombies, hide in the garage and pretend we know how to use tools, or, like Jeff Foxworthy said, have a beer and see something naked. We need these too, but mostly we need to enter life with our wives and kids. I'm not saying to work until midnight doing all her honey-do chores either. No matter how many things I do on my wife's list, there are twelve more things (I could care less about) written down right on their heels. The list never runs dry. She never rests, which is also wrong, but we need to work hard at this life of thistles and thorns...and then you can truly enjoy the fruit of your labor, take a deep breath, and pee off the back deck like a man should.

# DO YOUR DUTY

Yes, this means exactly what you think it means. For most of us men, this isn't an issue, especially when we are between twenty and forty years old. In fact, during our infertile years, I would come home and my wife would be standing in a garter belt and high heels saying, "We have to go right now!" Being the sacrificial husband I was, I always obliged. I was more than happy to take one for the team whenever my wife needed me to pitch in.

For other men who are older, stressed out, or just in the minority as far as the male mind is concerned, you'll have to make sure you pursue your wife and pursue her often. Now, she's going to act like she doesn't want to be chased, but she does. Ask any woman who is no longer pursued by her husband and she'll tell you it was way better to be chased all over the house than to be ignored. One time my wife was on the middle floor of a three-story house we were renting in Germany. For some reason my radar was up and running 100 percent the moment I stepped in the door. I started running up the stairs at Mach two for no reason. My wife started running to the next floor because she was stark naked for some reason. It matters not...I captured her and brought her back to the cave. Again, these were the early years. If I ran up a flight of stairs like that today, I would be on a heart machine shortly thereafter.

When I was first married, I thought we would be doing it three times a day. Ah, the rude awakening of married life. I had no problem doing my marital duty. Fast-forward twenty-plus years and I've slowed down a bit, yet every now and then, if she merely walks by and I get a whiff of per-fume, I am instantly ready. The difference today is that I'm good (I like to call it sexed up) for about a week at a time, whereas in my twenties I was good until about lunch time. Other men I have chatted with over the years say that sex just doesn't interest them that much, and of course they al-ways marry women who say they just can't get enough. (I always think the same thing you're thinking right now, but God knows what He's doing.)

If I had married a horndog woman who was as demented as I was back then, I would have never gone out of the house and worked. Most men are looking for "a lady in the streets and a freak in the sheets." Instead, however, you got the perfect woman God designed for you. And if two non-horndog types marry each other, there's no passion, little sacrifice, and even less growth. So what's the point? You need to be in the sack often, either as the initiator or the receiver or both. Eventually, no matter how sexual you feel or don't feel, if you keep the marriage bed empty too often, someone will be willing to take your place. It's been said that the devil spends a lot of his time trying to get you in bed before you should, and then once you're married, he does everything in his power to keep you out of it. Don't be that guy. You chase her and catch her until you're at least ninety. Use a cattle prod if you have to.

# BUY HER CARDS

Yes, cards are dumb, worthless, and a waste of money… to you. To women, however, it's not the card itself but what it represents. Once again, it's the fact that you thought of her that gets you good-boy points, not the cost of the card, and certainly not the picture on it. In fact, don't try to pick out just any card to scratch this one off your list; I tried it once and got caught. For some reason, women can tell if you took the time or not. It's like they all have this built-in feminine-missile warning radar that blurts out "fraud alert." And that reminds me of something else.

Get a card that's actually for her, not one that *you* like. For example, I like cards that say something funny, so I scour the shelves for the most sarcastic card I can find, with maybe a trout or an elk or something naked on it. On the inside of my soul, I tell myself I'm buying it for her, but really it suits me best. For some reason my wife doesn't enjoy nature like I do—through the crosshairs of a scope. And romantic cards just don't turn my crank, if you know what I mean. But every time I get her a funny card, she doesn't laugh. She's OK with it because at least I got her something, but it doesn't do much for her. Not only that, but romantic cards are a guessing game for me and almost always too cheesy for my liking.

Go with option C and get her a blank card. (Whoever thought of this one is a genius because the author writes absolutely nothing and we still by the things.) Anyhow, I like these better because I can say what I want. It is personal, genuine, and as mushy as she needs, and I can still be a little funny without ruining the moment. The fact that I took the time to write the card gets my wife all hot and bothered before she even reads it. (OK, I made that last part up, but it makes for a good man story.) The only way I can ruin it at this point is to write something in total sarcasm that she doesn't find at all funny. (I tried this too.) And don't be that guy who goes to Costco and buys a stack of fifty cards for two dollars…she'll know. They always know.

# BE HER HERO

I know you already think you're ten feet tall and bullet-proof. This means you are currently *your* hero for sure, but I said to be *her* hero. This is tough to do because you actually have to do something instead of flex in front of the mirror or work out more than one day a year. (Then there's Chris Rock, who said he packs a pistol wherever he goes out so he doesn't have to work out. I like it.) Being her hero requires a lot more action and a lot more character than we often display, however. Believe it or not, your wife actually believed all those romantic Disney cartoons growing up. And she didn't just dream this one time at the wedding, but she continues to dream this dream over and over again. She wants her knight in shining armor all the time, not some overweight dude eating chips on his beanbag asking for another beer. The reason many of those animated films say "they lived happily ever after" is because they always end right at the wedding.

What does it look like three, twelve, or twenty-five years into the marriage, though? Does she feel protected by you, or is she still the brunt of your jokes? Do you let family members (hers or yours) tear her down or gossip about her or talk ugly to her? The Scriptures are clear about this one: "For this reason a man will leave his father and mother and be united to his wife, and they will become one flesh" (Gen. 2:24). Do you let her family or the kids talk disrespectfully to her? Do you let bill collectors talk to her or are you the buffer? Do you make her work two jobs so you can have your fishing boat? (OK, that one is almost understandable.) You get the idea. You are one flesh; if someone hurts her, they are hurting both of you. You be her hero no matter who it is. She is your wife, no longer just a daughter or sister or anyone else's punching bag to be abused physically or verbally, so be ready to step in at every second.

One time my wife and I were loading groceries out of the car and into our small apartment. I parked close to the door, but for about ten minutes I was in a spot where I wasn't supposed to park so we could unload easier. Suddenly I heard some yelling outside. I ran outside to find some older guy (he was about forty back then) yelling at my wife about the car being parked where it was. I jumped in between him and my wife and told him if he had something to say that he was *only* allowed to talk to me. I didn't go off, but I let him know exactly how I felt about him yelling at my wife and that he better never do it again. He actually apologized. And more importantly, I had slain the dragon for my princess.

# KEEP YOUR SANITY

This means you do not have permission to freak out... ever. You can be upset. You can be irritated. You might even feel disrespected. But don't lose control, blow your top, and act like, "This time, she just went too far." I have watched wives tear up wedding photos in the middle of the night. I know of a husband who threw a coffee table through a window. A friend of mine took his wife all the way to the Grand Canyon and then turned around two miles before they got to the rim because he got mad at something stupid. I even kicked sand at my wife about twenty years ago, to my shame (some hero, huh).

My wife broke her hand swinging at me with all her might. The funny part (now) is that she hit my forearm, and that's how her hand broke. She screamed out in pain and immediately came to me, wanting my sympathy. On the outside I was being compassionate. On the inside I was thinking, "That's what you get for hitting this man's ICBM of steel. Of course you broke your hand. No fist can handle these iron pillars. In fact, I should have a security clearance just to carry these guns on the open street." My point is this: when you lose your cool, you are no longer in control. I don't care what the other person did or said. You may need to run for your life on occasion if she's waving a machete around, but keep your head (no pun intended) in all situations, at all times, no matter what.

That reminds me—watch your intake of alcohol. Just a couple years ago, I had to counsel a young man who hit his wife after drinking too many beers. He lost his mind and his career in the military because he lost control one time. My words to him were something like this: "She's your precious gem. You're supposed to hold her in the highest esteem. I have no sympathy for what you have done. You have become *that* guy. Never drink so much again so as to not have complete control over what you are doing. You violated your covenant." Anything that makes you lose your mind is wrong and needs to be weeded out of your life, be it alcohol, rage, drugs…or your mother-in-law.

# DON'T BE ROUGH

I used to have a tendency to play too hard with my wife and kids. Now don't get me wrong, we never used weaponry... OK, maybe a few plastic nunchakus and fourteen Nerf machine guns here and there, but nothing that would cause real injury. I had no intention of my son growing up to be a sissy, however. Once I saw him acting like a cowardly little schoolgirl, so I upped the ante in his life. I started rough-housing triplefold to toughen him up. And it worked. But the problem is that he started not enjoying our wrestling, punching, or chasing anymore. He started avoiding me, especially because I always made him earn his victories. My eleven-year-old (at the time) had been in and out of karate for five years, and I have to admit not all his victories were given to him as the next story illustrates.

One time I had to have gallbladder surgery due to it going belly up while I was in Iraq. About a week before I went to the hospital back in the United States, my son and I were play fighting when he jumped off the couch, hit me in the face with a pillow midair, and then kicked me right in the sternum. Then he finished off with a three-point landing straight out of *Crouching Tiger*. I fell over like a dead tree. He had brought down the old bull. As I sat there gasping for air in the fetal position, feeling like my last vital organ was about to pass through my butt, I could only muster a few words for him: "Good one, son; you got me." He was so scared he started crying. Although I couldn't speak, I was actually proud.

But then there's my wife and the point of our brotherly man-book here. She's actually somewhat violent herself due to her own childhood. She starts off playing, but then in a matter of seconds she's going for the jugular, sometimes with a Ginsu knife or whatever she can find nearby. (She needs to read my "never lose your mind" paragraph, I think.) And when I get hurt, I want to retaliate. I forget she's my wife, and all I see is my older brother. I turn back into a ten-year-old and use special warfare tactics only brothers can develop over years of latchkey-kid training. I don't want to hurt her ever, but I certainly don't want her to hurt me, so I've tossed in a little jujitsu and some genuine wrestling moves for good measure.

I can honestly say this has never helped our marriage— not one time. If I lose, I lose, and if I win, I lose. I have had to learn to play very, very mildly over the years and sometimes not at all. Every now and then I feel the blood start to rise and the Hulk inside about to erupt. In these moments, I have to take the lead and just cut off playtime. Recess is over. Otherwise it's "hammer time." If you are this guy as well, mellow out 100 percent or don't play at all. You owe it to your family to be such a man of strength on the inside that you never have to show it on the outside.

# MIND YOUR WORDS

You cannot say whatever you want or whatever you think just because it pops into your head. (I wish extended family would read that line daily for the next twelve years.) In fact, I will give you two concepts that should be included in all of your speech. One, you have to let your words be motivated by love, no matter what. Two, you have to speak the truth.

When she asks you if that outfit makes her butt look big, you might be tempted to say, "No, it's your thighs that make you look fat." This may be 100 percent true, but it's not a loving thing to say. If she asks you if you like her new haircut because she just chopped another foot of it off and she now looks like Harpo Marx, you have to figure out what you're going to say without crushing her. In this situation you should say something like, "I prefer your hair longer rather than shorter." Remember, you need love and truth.

If you say you love it when you really don't, you are lying, which isn't loving her, so find the balance between the two. If you are all truth in everything you say, you will be too harsh. Can you imagine if one of your kids brought home an art project and you said, "Man, that looks like crap! Just trying to be honest, son."

And speaking of truth, just because you think it doesn't make it true. How many times have we said something dumb like "you always" or "you never," even if it's the first time they ever did it? Stop and think before you speak; it will save you a whole lot of misery. I made the mistake (even though I thought it was true at that moment) of saying, "You're just like your mother." At that moment, I thought I was helping her see how she was being just like her mother. For some reason, my wife didn't really want my help that day. Truth is, I didn't need to spew it out of my mouth. And after adding an extra three hours of arguing, I realized I was the one who blew it. Being truthful in your own mind doesn't mean you should just go for it, especially if there's no love behind it.

One day I came home and popped off about the house being too cluttered and my wife spending too much money. It was 100 percent truthful (to me), but there was no love. I was bitter and gave a few quick rib shots right when I walked in the door. Stupid. I ruined the whole night, and what did I accomplish? Did my wife stop in her tracks and say, "You are so right. I'll cut our spending in half starting today and get right to cleaning something"? Hardly. Ask yourself if what you are about to say or do is really going to help or add fuel to the fire. The old rhyme that says "sticks and stones may break my bones, but words will never hurt me" is a big, fat lie. The Scriptures say words can tear down entire nations. Don't think for a second they can't tear down a marriage.

I love the old comedy routine from Rich Shydner where he and his wife were watching "Body Heat" with Kathleen Turner on the screen. His wife asked him if he thought Kathleen Turner was pretty. He said, "Yeah, definitely," and didn't think another thing about it. A couple hours later, he said, "Hey, babe, can you scratch my back?" She said, "Why don't you get Kathleen Turner to scratch your back?" Hear me, my brothers—truthful speech by itself will get you nowhere.

# BE THE MAN

Someone has to take the lead in your family. Don't believe all this new psychobabble garbage or women's liberation crap that has no basis in truth. When you go to work, someone has to call the shots, but everyone still has a role to exercise. When a sports team plays, someone tells them how they are going to score the points and how they can best defend themselves, but it always takes a team effort. Have you ever been to a carnival and seen the two-headed creatures? They are freaks of nature. We marvel at them for a few minutes and then go on our way. In fact, more often than not, these animals have very shortened life spans due to being so freaky and weird.

A marriage that has two heads is also a freak of nature, and it won't last that long. Anything with two heads eventually dies. How can you reach your goals and aspirations as a couple if neither of you or both of you are taking the lead at the same time? You, the man, need to be the leader of your family, period. God has called you to be the leader and it's an essential part of your manhood if you are married. Your wife may or may not like it, but you have to obey God.

I used to joke (actually, I still do) that there are four pillars to a man's heart: food, sex, sleep, and television. Basically, we can become little hamsters and just check out. Left to ourselves and our own desires, it's not far from the truth, but these aren't the true pillars God wants to cultivate in us. I love what Stu Weber wrote in his book *Four Pillars of a Man's Heart*: "When men are not men, a civilization falls. When men let their masculinity drift with the winds of culture, everyone loses. When a culture is castrated, it dies." He goes on: "What do you suppose masculinity was like when it was brand new? What did it look like? What did it smell like, just out of the box? How did it perform when it was newly awakened, so fresh from the heart of its Creator?"

What our leadership looks like today is where the discussions get juicy. Any man who does whatever he wants and does not take in the thoughts and input of his family is being foolish. One time my wife and I were trying to buy a mobile home (my wife's idea, by the way) as a place to live while we went to college. We had seen some really slick-looking trailers beforehand—one had a pair of skis holding the front door in place and another had thirty-seven ketchup stains on the carpet. Anyhow, she found this cute little single-wide and the family selling it wanted thirty-five thousand—dollars, not pesos. As we negotiated (we men, I mean), my wife, out of nowhere, pops off, "Will you take twenty-eight?" I told her as lovingly as possible to let me handle it…blah, blah, blah. They kind of laughed at us as we let ourselves out and went back to the dorm.

I then proceeded to lecture my wife about the ways of the world, real estate, and how men know how to handle property transactions without offending one another. The next morning the sellers simply said, "OK, we'll take twenty-eight." That was in 1994. We walked away from college with $10,000 in our pockets and no debt, mostly because of that trailer purchase. Since that time, my wife has chosen every single house of ours, one of which made me more money selling it than I made working the whole year. The bottom line is that my wife still has an eye for houses; I don't—I have an eye for watching money drift away or seeing too much remodeling work to do. She's the artist and can always spot the potential. She has made us thousands in real estate over the years, so where's my leadership in this area? Leadership here means letting her talents and abilities come forth like a spring of freshwater. In fact, my job is to nurture her talents, not squash them down like I tried the first time. And I'm the one who reaps the greatest benefits.

The opposite is also true, however. Don't allow anyone in your family to be responsible for something they suck at, unless you don't care about the final product. My wife is not allowed to do my editing—she stinks at it. I'm the grammar guy. I understand basic sentence rules, like you have to have a point, etc. Another example is in the financial realm. Usually, there is one person who can't save ten cents while the other person is the budget geek and bill payer—let them do the budget. It's not a fun job anyhow. One person just wants to "freak freely" and spend what you save anyhow—don't let them touch the spreadsheets. OK, they can touch the spreadsheets, but only give them a small cash allowance, never a credit card.

Of course there are thousands of things to lead at. Your job is to put the right people in the right places for the right reasons. Other times you just need to freaking do it because, as the man, God has made it your responsibility. For example, you need to take the spiritual lead in your family. Often, it is our women who are doing it. Wrong! You be the one to bring everyone to church, and you be the one who finds a church where everyone's needs are being met. You be the one to pray before meals and to take them on prayer walks. You be the one who takes the family to the soup kitchen to feed the homeless for a day. You be the one to read fantastic marriage manuals like this one. You get the idea.

# TURN IT OFF

I can't tell you how many times I have come home and it's all I can do to make it to the couch and let my soul leak onto the floor, drifting into a coma for three hours straight in front of the magic box. My genius is so tapped by the end of the day, it's all I can do to ignite the two working cranium cells that are still left (and one of 'em is piggybacking on the other for a ride). This is about the time my wife starts wanting help with the kids or setting the table. On the front end, her ideas sound like the most miserable things in the world. "This is my time," I think to myself. And then I start trying to use logic for some reason. "What did *you* do all day? How is the kitchen messy when no one was even home? Why do we even need to eat dinner; we had food yesterday? The kids can do their own homework; I was doing trig by the time I was four!" But the truth is this is *our* time.

We only get a short amount of time as a family, so why would I want to waste it flipping through two hundred channels? (Actually, it's nowhere near two hundred. Somehow, the cable company said that's how many I would get, but it's more like sixteen, seven of which are the same CSI show in different cities, complete with rock anthems to make them look cooler than they are; the other nine channels are infomercials with Chuck Norris working out or a solid product for curing ED.) And that's all I do is flip, flip, flip. So I decided to make some changes one year. I cut the cable. Can you believe those communists were charging me $179 a month for erectile dysfunction commercials? I don't even have it...yet. I decided I would rent a DVD every now and then, sometimes for the whole family and sometimes for just the wifey and me. This has cut down on the boob tube time quite a bit. At first it was kind of difficult, but then I found myself playing with the kids more, rolling around on the floor with our own version of WWE, helping with homework, and helping my wife pick up the house. (I'm still amazed that she and two kids can somehow destroy a house while I'm at work and they are supposedly at school.)

But such is life. It won't be long and those kids are going to be gone. There won't be any rolling around on the floor because there won't be any kids hanging around to do it. Sure, I can tackle the wife here and there (and throw my back out), but you can ask anyone who has been there, done that and they will tell you the best times in their lives occurred when the kids were young, life was chaotic, and Dad was trying to help his son with math he hadn't done himself in twenty-five years, Mama was in the kitchen, and the baby girl was trying to learn how to cook. Not once will you look back and say, "Remember that crime show we watched that one time?" Truth is you probably can't remember what you watched yesterday if you're like me. But I remember lots of family times to this day. I remember my family throwing biscuits at each other at the table. I remember eating the hair out of an artichoke heart and my father laughing at me. I remember grilling out on the patio with all six of us. I remember laughing until snot came out our noses. I'm creating our own snot memories with my own kids even now.

There are still some days where it's everything I can do not to collapse into the fetal position on my favorite chair. On these days, my wife and I have a signal (a dripping bodily meltdown, really) that says I feel like someone just got a running start and then kicked me in the face, so can I please bow out for the evening? She has been very gracious to me in this so far. My part is not to make this a nightly affair—I only get so many "coma cards," maybe one or two a month. So my encouragement to you is to be intentional about turning off the telly. There isn't anything good on anyhow, and like my wife always says, "Why do you want to live someone else's adventure?" Live your own life of chaos, my friend. This is your own reality show, and you won't regret it.

# CALL HER SOMETHING

I hear some guys call their wives "stinky," "the old lady," "the old ball and chain," "the other half," or simply "wifey." Sometimes it's worse than this, so if you have the issue of calling your spouse by horrible names, you need more help than this manual can offer. Remember when I said mind your words? Well, your terms of endearment matter even more. If your wife is a little overweight, you probably don't want to go with "my little orca," "chub chub," or "broccoli thighs" either. Find something that gladdens her heart; something that makes her feel built up and cherished; something that puts an actual deposit into her soul when she hears it. If you are unsure of what ministers to her heart, here's a really bizarre, wild thought—ask her.

For example, my wife likes to be called "Amazon temptress" and "love machine" whenever I have jungle music playing late at night. (OK, those are terms I like, and I'm trying to get her to jump on board. Oh, and there's no music, I just drifted into a fantasy land for a moment.) But she does like the more tender names of "my bride," "love," "Shnookums," "hot sweet," and sometimes "cream puff." Even when I'm ticked off, I find myself calling her "love," and she does the same for me, probably more out of habit at this point, but it still works. Now, the tone is somewhat different during an argument, but the titles we use are still positive. More about tones later.

The key is to use terms she likes all the time, not terms you *think* she likes or, worse, names you're trying to impress your buddies with. Often we are dead wrong about what our wives like and don't like because we focus on what we want or what we think is funny to our friends. We had newlywed friends a few years ago who called each other all kinds of names like "moron" and "stupid" as they playfully hit each other. It always looks innocent during year one, but wait until the couple has been married for fifteen years. Suddenly, one of the spouses realizes that he or she has been called some pretty insulting names over the years, and now it's starting to sound a little too truthful and hurtful. Our newlywed friends from back then are no longer wedded by the way.

So don't use your words carelessly. Do not call her something demeaning or something that's even neutral. Find a name that is positive and lifts her up. Trying to stay married and calling your spouse something she doesn't like is like driving your car with the horn engaged. Everyone sees you and hears you, but we wish we didn't have to.

# HONOR YOUR IN-LAWS

You don't know my in-laws, but let's just say they're different. Not just different from yours, I mean different from the rest of the world. I could go into great detail, but let me just share one little story so you get the picture. I was at my mother-in-law's house quite a few years back enjoying a brownie, as was my father-in-law. (They hadn't been married for several years, but we were all there for the holidays.) Anyhow, my father-in-law and I were stuffing our fat faces with several brownies when my mom-in-law pops off with, "By the way, those are Alice B. Tokeless." I had no idea what she was talking about and told her so. Looking at me like I was an idiot, she told me the brownies were made with marijuana. Several thoughts went through my head at that moment, since I could still think clearly before everything hit me. One had to do with the fact that I was regularly drug tested at my "prestigious" security guard job. (No, I wasn't a mall cop, but not too far off.) Secondly, my father-in-law was a recovering drug addict at the time and probably didn't need another trip to rehab. Third, who makes marijuana brownies for the family at holiday time and then tells everyone as crumbs are hitting the floor after your third one? And that was twenty-five years ago when they were somewhat normal. I have about 150 stories just like this that would blow your mind, but that isn't the point of this little blurb.

The point here is to honor your in-laws, even if they are bizarre, tick you off, interfere too much in your life, bring twelve dogs when they come to visit, or simply frustrate the living snot out of you as a form of retirement. Just honor them. I didn't say to cater to their every wish, like buy them each a car and a house every Easter. I didn't say let them run your marriage, your family, or your decisions. (For those of you who do, I will say more about this later.) In fact, you should seek their input, but in the end you had better be running your own family no matter how weird yours used to be. Honoring your in-laws means you don't shame them, yell at them, talk down to them, put them down, or even avoid them. That hasn't helped anyone since the beginning of time, and it won't help your jacked-up in-laws either. (By the way, we are all jacked-up to some degree.) So don't dishonor them in front of them or behind their backs; honor is honor, especially when the grandkids are around.

Don't get me wrong, I have rules I have to lay down in order to visit most of our family or for them to visit me. For example, you can't bring drugs to my house or my nine-year-old might accidently take your stash. If you borrow my car, please bring it back—I still need it for work on Monday.

If you are going to test out a boat's seaworthiness, that's fine—just don't take my kids along with you until I know it actually floats. If I take you to dinner, don't order the lobster and sea bass platter when everyone else is having a corndog. It's a fine line and sometimes difficult for me to know what to do, so I always ask the question, "Does what I am about to say or do bring honor or dishonor to them?" Honor them out of who God has called you to be at the moment, not because they deserve it.

# LET PARENTS GO

S ince I was just writing about in-laws, I have to go with
the parental chat also for a moment. It's your job to take
charge and care of your family, not your mom and dad's.
If you had the guts to get married, you've taken on a new
role, and you shouldn't be expecting your parents to bail
you out physically, financially, mentally, or any other "ly" I
can think of. Again, you can and should seek their advice if
they are the kind of people who have a proven track record.
(Why would you ask marital advice from folks who have
been married and divorced five times? On the same note,
don't seek financial advice from someone who has to borrow from you every other week and owes $52,000 on credit
cards.)

Parents are no different; they are very wise with some
things and very unwise with others, just like you and me.
And this may be a shock to some of you, but your parents

may be 100 percent wrong on some things. But here's the bottom line: your mom and dad already raised you, and it's now your turn. If anything, we men should have learned from their mistakes and should be ready to pass on even greater increases for the next generation, but you can't do that if you're still hanging on to your parent's coattails.

Like in-laws, you should honor your own parents, but don't let them run your life. This is how we get "mama's boys" today, and I don't mean sissies. These are the men who have moved out physically but haven't cut the emotional and psychological umbilical cords from Mama. I can't tell you how many times my wife and I have been teaching marriage studies and one of the men spits out something absurd. When I ask where they got the idea, it almost always comes from Mom, Dad, or both. Every time there's a little spat in the relationship, these men call Mom or Dad to get some sympathy. Some parents will shoot straight with their kids; some just take the son's or daughter's side automatically because "their little precious" can do no wrong. Really... you should have seen "your little precious" throwing knives at his or her spouse last week!

In fact, my wife and I don't even tell our parents anything anymore because it always makes them dislike the other spouse. If you want some solid marital advice, go find a couple that's been married about ten years longer than you. If they truly care about you as a couple, they will tell you the truth about your marriage and how to treat each other if you let them. The beauty is, they aren't related to you, so they have more of an objective view than parents will. They can call you on your crap and yet keep from offending you if you stay teachable.

# KEEP IT PURE

Brace yourself—I'm stepping on serious toes now. So you've been looking at porn for quite some time now. I know it, and you know it. Some of you are a little more subtle—you just stare at the underwear ads for hours or pretend to be looking at Victoria's Secret to buy your lady an outfit. (It would fit in your own shirt pocket it's so skimpy). Some of you are so deep in it you can't see straight. Others are just dabblers. Still others have prostitutes and "friends" you see regularly as you go about your daily facade. All I can tell you is that you are killing your marriage little by little. Destruction from the inside, and trust me, I know all about it. I finally broke free from all the smutty stuff not that many years ago. (All it took was a deployment to Baghdad, Iraq, to get through to me.) Many of you haven't broken free yet. I know that God made women the hottest things in the world. I know how you think, and no, it's not our fault that we think that way naturally. However, we can change how we think, and we can certainly choose not to act on those thoughts.

To this day my wife still doesn't quite understand the male mind. It's been said that a man thinks about sex once every seven seconds…and that's only because he lies about the other six. All I can tell you is to be loyal all the time; only have eyes for her. As Mark Driscoll has said many times, "Be a one-woman man." This means you don't get all bug-eyed when watching television. (OK, well, my son does, but that's because I don't let him watch very much of it.) In fact, you may want to choose movies that are appropriate to watch in front of Grandma (unless your grandma is worse off than you). Watch which magazines you "stumble upon" in the magazine racks. Really watch the small flirtations that start when you're at work. Be careful of "coincidently" driving by the university when cheerleading practice starts every day at 2:00 p.m. We men have to watch our wandering eyes in every setting, all day, every day. We're sneaky. We can even fool ourselves into "accidently" seeing things we shouldn't. Sometimes it's innocent, but oftentimes it's not. To be the kind of man I'm talking about, you have to put up your own defenses long before the attacks come your way. Plan for the battle before going outside. It isn't a matter of *if* but *when* you're going to be attacked by the lure of a woman.

I have a friend, for example, who struggles with porn so much he won't even walk down grocery store aisles that have magazine racks. He has Internet access, but only his wife has the password to unlock the various content. Another friend can't even watch the Discovery channel; if he sees animals doing things, he wants to act like an animal too.

I believe he coined his behavior "drunk monkey sex." And these are all things they've put in place because they know who they really are at their cores. Where do you fall short? What kind of defenses do you have in place to keep your mind, life, and marriage pure? Put on your armor ahead of time.

# CLEAN YOURSELF UP

It is a known fact that women have a more highly developed sense of smell than us men. That being said, don't confuse their bionic abilities with normal man stink. Take my twelve-year-old Durango, for example. Be it workout clothes, sneeze and snot spackled about, coffee spills, a little leftover Taco Bell, or man gas that has permanently stained my driver's seat, my rig has a natural manly aroma that I'm quite proud of. This is expected in a real man's world. (Just check your side of the bed and your pillow as option number two if you don't believe me.) But this is different than the extra green clouds of putrid goodness we often create for those around us.

A few years ago, my two female office mates were complaining about another man's presence. They had both verbalized that he "stinks like onions and armpits." Trust me, guys, women can smell you 150 yards away if you aren't wearing cologne, a pound of deodorant, and you haven't recently gargled with a quart of Listerine. So if you want to spruce things up around your house, forget about putting an air freshener near the toilet and start with your own nasty body. If you're one of those guys who thinks he can go two or three days without showering or brushing your teeth, guess what...you can't. Even other dudes can smell you, which is saying something. And this is just the smells piece.

Women like us to look good too. We aren't the only ones who are visual, you know. Men are primarily stimulated by what their eyes see, but this doesn't mean women have zero eyesight. For example, if every time your wife looks at you Saturday morning just after breakfast, you have the five o'clock shadow going already, your teeth still aren't brushed, and your hair looks like you combed it with an eggbeater, trust me, she can see you...and she isn't turned on. (And this is disregarding the fact you tried to pick out your own clothes again.) You aren't the cool, unshaven, messy-haired GQ guy on the magazine cover. You probably look homeless.

We need to look good for our ladies and at least do the basic grooming every single day. We all have those days, of course, when "it just isn't going to happen today." I had one of those days the other day and went to kiss my daughter good night. I hadn't brushed my teeth all day because I was busy "doing stuff." Right after I kissed her good night, her seven-year-old already-developed womanly senses took over, and in her little, sweet, brutally honest voice, she simply said, "Daddy, you smell like dogfish." I could immediately picture it and therefore smell it.

The message of a man's need to clean himself up had once again passed to the next generation, only this time it was for a future wife and mother who may one day be tortured by another man's stink. Now that I think about it, maybe I should just eat out of the dog bowl and then chew on a trout with raw onions and tell my daughter that every boy smells exactly like this whenever he tries to kiss you. That should keep her away from them for a few more years anyhow.

# TAKE HER DANCING

When I write the ongoing sequel about things women can do for us men, I'm going to tell the wives to take their husbands on a good elk hunt at least twice a year. Unfortunately, this is a manual about how we can minister to our wives, so you have no leg to stand on. (In fact, if you ever met me in person, you'd know I have virtually no legs to stand on at five foot four.) Let's face it—most men hate dancing. For one, most men cannot dance. It's a biological and physiological fact. Why would a man go put himself on public display to prove it? Secondly, even if we do exhibit a little rhythm here and there, it doesn't mean we actually like it.

Women, however, love it. Something in their genes (and their jeans) makes them have to shake it all the time. I thought it would go away after the kids came along, but no such luck for me. (If you are married to a woman who dislikes dancing, consider yourself fortunate and move along to the next paragraph.) And we know our ladies love it because we used to go to the dance clubs pretending to be there for our enjoyment. In reality, it was the hunt and capture we were after. It's like real hunting today. I don't go into the woods because I happen to like the woods. I'm there for the kill. (I do like being in the trees, but stay focused with me.) We went dancing to "bag it and drag it back to the cave." Women go dancing because they genuinely like to dance. Unthinkable, but it's the truth, so here's what you need to do, and it's also the toughest part.

How do you (even if you loathe dancing) take your partner out somewhere she can allow herself to "freak freely"? This is difficult to answer because you certainly aren't going to take her to the raunchy places *you* used to go. You are older now, more mature, and your choices are limited. I have only found a couple places I can take my wife now, but she loves both of them, so it all counts. One is to go country line dancing, and the other is to go ballroom dancing. Now before you throw up in your mouth a little, hear me out. I'm not one of those guys who have natural rhythm, but both of these options have real dance steps a man can actually memorize and perform. For this reason alone, they have my vote. If you're really lucky, you may be able to get brownie points merely by taking a line dancing class with your wife. This way, everyone in the room looks just as retarded as you do. (Sorry if you don't like the term *retarded*, but there really is no other way to explain the lack of our dancing skills.) The essential piece is to take her somewhere she can dance that isn't a meat market. You need to go somewhere you won't get shanked in the parking lot and somewhere everyone keeps their clothes on so the marriage stays intact when you get back in the car to go home.

One word of caution, however. I went to a wedding with my wife about two years ago as of this writing. Since I live in Colorado, this wedding happened to be at a lodge in Breckenridge—a small town about ten thousand feet above sea level. Sure enough, Lady Gaga came on during the reception, and my wife gave me that look, implying we should be a part of the festivities. I knew I hadn't taken her dancing for quite a while, so I grabbed her by the hand (in my normal manly fashion) and dragged her to the dance floor like I was going to show her a thing or two. I was about to bring sexy back, when about halfway through the song, due to the elevation and my general lack of exercise that year, I started to feel dizzy and was running out of breath. It was all I could do to hang on as "Poker Face" rattled through my head. As my wife spun in circles and danced about, I tried everything not to collapse and prove to her my youth had left me...apparently in just twelve months.

Here's the moral of the story, my friends: take the dance classes with her. It's a win-win because you'll look better by not falling into a coma, and she'll still be able to "get jiggy with it."

# SHE'S NO DOORMAT

For those of you still confused about your proper leadership role, read the earlier entry called "Be the Man." There's nothing wrong with being the head of the house; in fact, you're supposed to be. But what I've found is that most men don't know how to be the head of the home without being a big, fat, pain-in-the-butt jerk-tyrant at the same time. (Sounds like some military bosses I've worked for in the past.) There's always an issue with making the tough call when every single person in your family is against you. That one's tricky, so you better have more information, prayer, and counsel than everyone else before you go with your grand decision. (Usually, we men don't want to seek counsel because we know anyone with a smidge of wisdom will probably tell us we're full of crap.) If, however, you're making a decision and everyone is in opposition, you need to first remember that God has called us all to peace. Secondly, we are supposed to consider our spouse's wishes above our own. There is a problem, however, with treating your wife like a big pile of doo-doo, no matter what you decide.

You don't get the luxury of yelling. You can't be un-kind...ever. I know we all fall short in this area, but this is where the bar has been set by God, not you. And why do I write this? Because I have friends who treat their dogs bet-ter than their wives and children. Have you ever been yell-ing at your wife one second, and then the phone rings and you have the softest, nicest voice of all only ten seconds later? That's because you are making a choice to be kind to the stranger on the phone. This means you have full control over how you treat your wife, no matter what she hit with the car or bought with the credit card or didn't clean well enough for your liking. The relationship is al-ways more important than whatever you're freaking out about. Remember that.

Take last night as an example. My wife decided to start a WWE match with me at 2:30 a.m. For whatever reason, she still thinks she can take me in these UFC bouts. All I did was slide her direction in the bed until she had about three millimeters of surface to hold on to before tumbling to the floor. My sweet, innocent angel kept trying to pinch me, punch me, and even bite me. Every time she did, I inched her closer and closer toward the pit of lava on the floor. (My vast training from my older brother and years of wrestling and jujitsu had kicked in.) I gave one final warning before fate and gravity kicked in. She didn't listen. But being the gentleman I'm trying to be, I held on to her and lowered her three feet to the floor in a fluff of blankets, sheets, and thirty-two throw pillows. She's the one I love and cherish, so even in our battles, I treat her like the lady she is. You need to do the same.

# ASK HER FORGIVENESS

L et's face it: we all have serious room for improvement as human beings. Now before you get all freaked out and go down the road of how perfect God created us, remember that we have plenty of bad things about us as well as good. I'm just talking about the bad for a moment, and this one in particular is extremely hard for men to do. Yet our wives need to hear it more desperately than we do. Don't get me wrong, we men need forgiveness as much as our wives, but they need to hear it twice as much as we do. I hope you get that. I'll say it again: they need to hear it twice as much as we do. If my wife does something wrong to me, 99 percent of the time she can make up for it right then and there by giving me a simple hug, a small kiss, and certainly with a flash of some body part (and I don't mean an elbow). That always makes it better.

Wives are a different breed, however. (I tried flashing her once when she was angry...I didn't get quite the response I had hoped for.) And my wife in particular adds a pound of salt to my shame and misery. When I do something wrong, she only likes to hear an apology that goes something like this (caps added for the pain and anguish I feel just typing it): I AM SORRY. THAT WAS DEAD WRONG. WILL YOU FORGIVE ME? Can you imagine what that's like for a man? A sharp stick in the eye is easier. But I will tell you this: it releases her anger and pain immediately, particularly because I used the exact words she has requested, and she knows the suffering I'm enduring just to repeat it. Usually she just smiles when I say that phrase, and everything is happy again.

Where I struggle is when she wants me to ask forgiveness for something that I didn't necessarily do. One time my foot slipped off the brake pedal, and she got scared. She started telling me I needed to ask forgiveness for that. ("Are you smoking crack?" I thought.) We went round and round, and I finally said, "I'm not apologizing for that." I had no problem saying, "I'm sorry that scared you," or "Sorry you were scared by that." She wanted me to say I was sorry. (Can you see the big fat finger pointing at my forehead?) She thought we should seek outside counsel to see who was right. One point finally went to the husband. (First one in fifteen years, so I took it.)

That being said, there are plenty of opportunities for you to ask for forgiveness if you are alive and breathing. You and your spouse are both going to do things to hurt each other, and you need to fix it when you do. You're going to have to ask your wife what she needs from you and then give it to her when you do her wrong. The point is you have to be willing to step out and genuinely seek her peace, one-ness, and favor again. Isn't that what forgiveness is all about anyhow? The beauty is she has to receive it. Since we are saying what they requested, they can no longer look for justice or repayment of some kind (like the silent treatment)— unless you broke something sentimental of hers. The slate becomes clean and you both get to start fresh again, which is nice, because twenty minutes later you'll be in the dog-house again if you talk.

# TALK TO HER

Comedian Rich Shydner says, "Sometimes we forget to do little romantic things with our wives...like talk to them." We flap our lips all day at work, either in person, on e-mail, or on the phone, and then we come home totally spent. She's been with the kids all day and she's ready to let it all out and have some adult conversation. Instead, you turn on the tube and watch some news, a good game, or maybe an episode of *Glee* if you've already torn up your man card. Eventually you stuff your fat face at dinner, go back to the television, and then tinker around in the garage because that's what men are supposed to do. The night ends and you haven't said three words to her except, "Pass the salt." Of course, two hours later when you think it's time for her to fulfill her marital duty, you spit out how beautiful she is twenty seconds before making a mad dash to the bed, where you wait patiently to "finish off" your day. She doesn't want anything to do with you because you haven't connected with her. Now you're mad, and on and on the cycle goes.

This goes on until one day someone else really talks to her, listens to her, and interacts with her. She wanted this from you, but you weren't willing because you were "so tired" night after night. As I have already said, you can have "one of those days" when it's all you can do to breathe in and out by yourself and then go to bed, but it better not be the norm. And by the way, going to the movies does not count as talking time. I know, because I just tried this a couple years back on Father's Day. My wife tried to spend time with me and talk to me while I was watching the movie. One, I was watching *Thor*, so no talking was allowed in my mind. Two, it was Father's Day—my day. Three, I am not physically capable of watching a movie *and* talking. I can do one, not both. (One penguin on the iceberg at a time, remember?) Four, she isn't interested in any of the new Marvel or DC Comics hero movies, and I like all of them. So I halfway listened to her and halfway watched my movie. The following day, we went out to the theater again. (Two days of movies in a row; I didn't know what to do with myself.) We went to a late movie, didn't like what was playing, and went next door to the only other movie available—*The Avengers*! Even though God Himself had sided with me that night by giving me the sequel, my wife still wanted to talk. I'd thought we'd had two great dates in a row, but I'm good at lying to myself. I had failed miserably. I hadn't talked for two hours straight as both firing synapses were apparently already occupied.

Men, we have to be intentional about talking to our wives. I have to be intentional about helping her get dinner ready, intentional about helping her clean up, and intentional about getting the kids to bed. Then we usually have about an hour window before I start drifting into la-la land. This is our best (and usually only) time. Some days, she doesn't need "tune time," as we call it. (That's where we tune into one another.) I can go days with zero conversation and not think a thing of it. She's OK with taking a day off here and there when she's painting the toy room, talking on her cell phone, and combing the cat at the same time. I like those nights too because I get to go vegetate on the couch. But what I don't want is for her dreams to go unfulfilled and feel like she's married to a "dead horse," as she puts it. I want her to know she is loved and valued and that I want to know her deepest longings in life, even if it's just talking about what the kids ate for lunch and which one peed on the floor that day.

# ALWAYS PROTECT HER

This takes many forms, but at a minimum, you should protect her physically and emotionally. (I can't protect her financially because she is usually the monster.) Protecting her physically should be natural to most men, although I have seen instances where the husband was actually the main perpetrator and took out his aggression on his wife and kids. (Sometimes my wife and I have small UFC bouts, but I always try to make sure she doesn't hurt me.) Other times, it is the husband who is just plain mean. He's the one who has the anger problem. He's the one who is cursing and yelling all the time. He's the one who tells her she isn't worth anything and the kids will never turn out to be anyone of value. If this is you, stop reading this and go get some help. If you're like most men, and I know us well, you aren't going to seek help. You're going to make it miserable for you, the kids, and her for the next fifteen years and then remarry and start your same old crap with a new person. Here is your chance, on the front end, to do something about it.

My suggestion (if you're the subtle type of jerk and not the type who goes as far as kicking the dog and throwing logs in your spare time) is to find some small group to attend. Go to church, find a good marriage group (with people you actually like), and go every single week. Yes, I said go to church, you big sissy. A manual isn't going to do it for you. Men need other good men to hang around, period. If you can't find a good group, do what I did—start one.

Sometimes it's the wife who is the abuser. Take my wife, for example. She came from a home where she saw alcohol, drugs, and all the lovely stuff that usually accompanies that. So when we got married at the ripe old ages of eighteen and twenty, we had some learning to do. She would get mad, do a half gainer triple twist over the dining room table, and try to kick me in the mouth. (OK, I'm exaggerating…it was actually the coffee table.) I already mentioned how she broke her hand trying to hit my forearm of steel, but I still have a responsibility in all of it. I am her protector.

No matter what, you need to protect her from anyone and everyone, including other women. I have often heard it said that men should never hit women. I have added this caveat: if you are physically attacking anyone in my family, I will punch you in the face…even if you are a lady. A couple times I have seen women foaming at the mouth, and every man reading this knows what I mean. They can be more ruthless than men on occasion. I have had to hang up on women and write pretty blunt e-mails to chicks that were hell-bent on wounding my wife with their words. One woman not too long ago told my wife I was controlling. Really? Maybe I'm just protecting my bride from people like her, and I don't apologize. So in your face...I mean, book!

And this protection definitely includes family members. In fact, I might argue that most of the time, it is our own families that do the bulk of the wounding. To all the loving families out there, we men will take you out if we need to. My wife doesn't like me to jump in her business all the time, but I do it anyway because no one is going to hurt or talk like that to my spouse, even family. (Only I get to do the abusing!)

She can handle her own battles for sure, but one thing I really took to heart a few years ago is that my wife and I really are one flesh. If someone is deriding her, they are deriding me, and we are one team, stronger together. If they hurt her, they hurt us. Like Ecclesiastes says, "Two are better than one" and "Though one may be overpowered, two can defend themselves." So I stick up for her. That's one of my jobs. Her friends and family don't always like it, but that's my choice, my family, and my wife. I will have to stand before God some day and defend my actions, or lack thereof, and I choose to protect her all day, every day. You should too.

# HAVE NO CONDITIONS

When you love a person, it has to be unconditional. Your emotions and feelings come and go all the time, but if you truly want to love someone, you do what you are supposed to do regardless of where your head's at. (And your head can be in a variety of places.) Your relationship is more than wedlock—it is also a padlock, something to be kept under lock and key, where you do the right thing no matter how much you want to lose it and break free.

My wife and I had a little tiff a while back. And it was little, but enough to still make my psyche hurt. While I was still angry at her, I went down to the Starbucks and got her a chai tea (her favorite) and myself a quadruple shot mocha (so I could think about what I wanted to say while the caffeine was still fresh). I failed in that I didn't tell her where I was going (I probably did it on purpose if one were to search the deep recesses of my soul), but the point is the same. I love her through my actions (one of them anyhow) despite my frustration. In fact, the only thing that made my anger dissipate was listening to a good sermon later in the morning. We still hadn't resolved anything, yet I opened the car door for her later on as well. Sounds like I'm bragging, but that isn't my intention. Let your actions always be unconditional and not related to what you feel. You can always talk about what's ticking you off when the time is right and you're not in the heat of battle.

And speaking of being ticked, I saw a pattern as of another morning yet again. We had another minor tiff, this time about how to celebrate the holidays, with in-laws or friends or a combination of each—funny how this same issue comes up every so many years (only not funny because it isn't resolved yet). When we and family lived in different states it still caused tension, but now that we're all the Griswold family in one spot, you would think it would have gone away—it hasn't. I'm sure I'm not alone.

My first thought was to drive away for Thanksgiving to a very lonely lake, rent a pontoon boat, and fish for the holidays. No anger or squabbling with trout, pike, and salmon. No drama. The biggest decision for the day would be what kind of bait I wanted to try. Then reality set in. Leaving my kids and wife for Thanksgiving Day wasn't really the best idea. Strange where your mind can go, huh? This is a solid reason why we need other men (and manuals) in our lives that point us in the right direction when we are acting in total stupidity.

So once again, I went for a prayer walk and listened to one of my favorite speakers, Greg Laurie, just an hour later. Of course, in Godlike timing, his message was about having a real commitment to your spouse and that even he, after thirty-seven years of marriage, still has issues that arise. Now, you can look at that and say, "Wow, that blows to still have problems after that much time" or "Wow, I'm in good company." We will always have issues, but the right attitude is working it out and plugging along until the next issue comes up...which will be tomorrow.

# NEVER AND ALWAYS

I hate it when couples use words like *never* and *always*. (I never do that.) Let me change that first sentence—I hate it when my wife and I say it the most. We say things like this: "You never clean up the dishes." "You always have something sarcastic to say." (That is only 88 percent true, so ha!) "Your mother is always in our business." These are two words you need to filter from your vocabulary, even if there's some truth to them. The only thing we always do is poop and sleep. I never throw away bread either…there are starving people in Pueblo.

For one, they're a curse. When someone hears they are always like this or that, it verbally confirms something in the soul that encourages one to maintain the status quo. It is a self-fulfilling prophecy. You will actually bring about what you detest even more so. If your real goal is to help your spouse not be like what you are describing, stop using *never* and *always*. A better way to describe something might be, "Hey, I'm noticing a pattern in your life. I just realized that your underwear has been hanging on the bedpost for the last three weeks, and the dog is kind of afraid of it. Would you mind tossing them into the clothes basket when you have a free minute? Thanks, honey. You're a true woman."

Secondly, it isn't ever 100 percent true. While she may frequently spend more money than you bring in and often drive faster than the posted speed limit, it isn't always. Though she may rarely check the gas gauge or forget to tell you, "Wow, you are an epic warrior. I'm surprised you aren't a world-class fighter instead of working in your cubicle," it isn't an *always* or a *never* necessarily.

# SOMETHING'S ALWAYS
# BROKEN

If your house is like mine, seventeen things break or need fixing at the same time—usually when it's blowing snow sideways. Sometimes they wouldn't have needed fixing if my wife had simply asked me ahead of time. Take the fact that she locked herself out the other day. No problem if it were the outside of the house, but oh no, she was locked out of our own bedroom. Men know the secrets: we know to push the little button inside the hole; we'll take the door off the hinges if need be; we even know how to trick the door. Not at my house. My wife is mostly about speed because she has another agenda. She immediately went around the outside to go through the window because she realized it was still open. Never mind there was a screen still in the way; she simply folded it in half (metal frame included) and climbed in. Brownie points for being unafraid. She gets mass deductions for causing irreparable damage—that's usually my job. So our bedroom door lock is now fixed, but the screen looks like a taco draped in front of the glass…real nice and redneck-like! One project down, three more added.

My wife and I have an agreement (unwritten, of course): I have agreed to help her with one project every night during the week to complete my manly household duties, so she must choose wisely. Oh, and after-dinner dishes don't count as a project. I realize it's kind of crass, but she's fond of saying, "Doing dishes is like wiping your butt: it just needs to be done without being asked." I'm talking about hanging a curtain rod or overhauling the kitchen cabinets by bedtime. Sometimes I do more than one project, but if your wife is like mine, there are thirty-four items she wants done every single day. I don't know where she comes up with these things either. Fixing something that previously worked makes perfect sense, but new things like shampooing the cat, watering the yucca plant, or staining the kids' outside fort just doesn't resonate with my soul.

Plus, the woman doesn't actually sleep, so her list grows and grows by the hour. My other rule is that I want to be done with all mystery projects by 8:00 p.m.—no six-hour projects (during the week) like fixing the SUV transmission ten minutes before I'm running out the door.

The point is that you married a woman, and a woman wants things fixed around the house so she doesn't feel like she lives in a shack. (You may actually live in a shack, but just don't let her feel that way.) Whatever roof is over your head, make it her castle. Keep it looking nice and taken care of. When you take care of the house, you are taking care of her. When the house looks good, she feels good. When the rafters sag, you sag.

# KEEP THE PEACE

This one is going to be really easy to write about and difficult to carry out, but here goes. Every time you and your wife have a little fight (or a large one, for that matter), *you* be the one to initiate making up. Don't be too quick about it, however, or you might get shanked. But after a little simmer time, you be the one to make the peace first. You are the man of the house, right? Do you even know what being a man is? It means you get to take all the responsibility. This doesn't mean you are the only one at fault, but it does mean you get to take the heat for how well your marriage is going or not going. That's your job...one of them, anyhow. This means it's your job to make the first move. Man was designed and created to be the initiator, so congratulations on being the head of your household. Now man up—every single time things go south.

I did the opposite once...once. My wife and I were fighting about twenty years ago now, and I did the manliest thing ever...I went to sleep in the other room after a huge fight. You know what woke me up? My wife hauling off and punching me in the spine as hard as she could. (She's not proud of this, but I have her permission to share her failure to illustrate mine.) Do you see where making peace would have been the better option? Not only would we have reconciled before bed that night, I would have a better posture to this day and still be able to tie my shoes.

# YOUR DRIVING SKILLS

Stop driving like a maniac! You aren't Mario Andretti, and your wife hates it when you threaten her life and the lives of your children. You think you have a little *Fast and Furious* in your blood, but really it's more Ford and flatulence. If you want to be a man, learn to drive like an old lady.

My mentor once told me that his insurance was less than mine, and not because of his quicker reflexes. He assured me that my youth actually allowed me to have much faster reflexes and responses to crises than he ever manifested. The reason my insurance premiums were higher than his was due to my statistical lack of judgment. For example, when I looked at a wooden ramp leading up a thirty-foot riverbank with a twist at the tail end, I thought to myself, "I've seen *Dukes of Hazzard*. I can probably make the jump." So I went for it. My mentor knew better. And now I do too.

Trust me—you can't make the jump. And if you think you can, you should only attempt it when you're by yourself...let the family live. I never did attempt the jump. I did at one point (as an all-knowing sixteen-year-old) drive through a four-foot hedge near a McDonald's doing about 30 mph in a Jeep CJ-5. Hedge...one point; judgment...zero.

Secondly, stop getting so freaking mad at other drivers. You do the same thing every time you get on the road. Why? Because they are basically you. And your anger hasn't changed another driver in twenty-five years, has it? No one drives as good as you do, right? Unlike you, other people don't know what to do at a four-way stop. Other people always cut you off. Other people drive too slowly in the fast lane. Only other people turn without using a signal. Only an idiot would drive while distracted and using the phone. You have never and would never do these things.

You haven't gotten in any accidents, you say...but you probably caused seven. Face it—these people are going to be out there every single time you get in the car. (Like I said, you're one of them.) Plan on it. Be ready. Think about how to respond ahead of time. No cussing. No bullets (unless it's a California freeway). No middle fingers. No arm waving. No "solid" eyebrows. And this is just on the way to church...wait until Monday. Just smile and know that "you" are everywhere out there. It's not about you; it's about those inside the car next to you. Your family will think you a much better man if you pull it together *before* you take them on the road.

# LEARN TO FIGHT

Too often we fight about the dumbest things, and half the time, even when we're arguing over something, we aren't even talking about the real issue that made us angry in the first place. Let's say you get a crazy idea one day and decide it's a golden opportunity to have a discussion about her punctuality—mostly because she has none. You two have been late to every function you can think of for the last several years now, so you decide to launch the attack because it's fresh in your mind. Fast-forward a few minutes and you are criticizing her mother, making a sarcastic remark about her cooking, and then you finish it off with a comment about the pigsty you currently live in. You just failed. You've been there; I've been there. Let's do this right. Stick to the issue. I was told by a mentor once to write the issue down on a napkin or piece of paper and put that napkin on the table. This gives you a visual to stay on topic and stay focused. Wives run down rabbit trails too, but this is our man-to-man time, so stick to the issue.

Secondly, to fight right, you need not really fight at all. This is supposed to be a discussion, so say what's on your mind; remain the cool manly man you are made to be and stay chill. I had a friend once (trust me, it really was a friend) who got so sick of his wife making him late, that he left her and the baby crying in the driveway as he sped off—wait for it—to church. His words were basically this: "Being late to church is the worst of all lateness because now you are wasting God's time." Wow. Apparently you can waste your husband's time, but God's…nope. Yes, it's true; Jesus hates the wife's lateness more than anything else. Speak the truth in love like I already stated. Speak your mind, but with grace and gentleness. This isn't a shouting match or a competition. It's both of you trying to understand.

Third is your timing. Don't start a fight because it just occurred to you. Did your spouse just lose her job, find the dog drowned in the pool, and then run into the ditch on the way home? Not a good time for you to bring up your need for more sex in your life. I like it best when my wife warns me ahead of time. She often says, "I need to talk with you when you have a minute." I try not to roll my eyes and think, "What now?" The nice part is this gives me time to think about what she could possibly need now, especially with such a wonderful man on her hands, doing all that I already do. In any case, once I come down from the other crises in my life, I'm eventually ready to listen to her real needs.

The second you notice the tones starting to get ugly, the volume getting too high, or that you aren't even talking about the issue any more, just stop. Regroup and reattack later. Stick to the issue. Stay loving. Speak truthfully. Leave her mother out of it. (Don't completely forget about your extra sex needs.)

# DON'T CLAM UP

I hear over and over again that wives want us husbands to open up and tell them what's really on our minds. First of all, we men know darn well women don't really want to know what we're thinking because half of it wouldn't even make sense. They do want to know us; we just don't want them to know how bizarre our thoughts really are. One time my wife asked me what I was thinking about after a long period of silence. When I revealed to her it was mostly a deep inquiry in my soul about Bigfoot and other undiscovered monsters still lurking around the Rocky Mountain region, she wasn't really interested. More importantly, I think she was wondering who the heck she had married...and this was just a couple weeks ago.

As I have said many times, if you were to pan into my skull at any given moment, there's a good chance you would see a clown on a unicycle going around in circles. Thank you, US Army, for killing off most of my thinking capacity. Anyhow, it is our job as men to find a way to open up...something...anything for our wives. I've heard a lot of dumb things over the years that don't help whatsoever, like, "Minds are like parachutes; they only work when open." Isn't that inspiring? No, it isn't. It's also been said not to be so open-minded that your brains fall out. Now we're banging on all four cylinders.

That being said, here's the point. We need to allow our wives access to the deepest parts of our souls—even if they're only two millimeters deep. I know you don't think you have a deep part, but you do, and it's not just your nasal cavity. You were made in the image of God, so it's in there; maybe you just haven't tapped into it yet. Maybe you need to do some excavating and unearth some things—and it might take a little work. This is the part you need to explore, take a jackhammer to, split open with a pickax, whatever...let her find out what's in there (besides the lint and leftover Doritos).

This is the stuff your wife is most interested in—not your golf game, the giant colossal squid finally caught on camera, or even the latest things at work that took 90 percent of your day. Sure, she'll listen to that stuff if she has to, but that's not what she's after. It's just like when you come home and you're feeling a little...you know...frisky. She starts talking about kids, puke on the doorknob, the variety of poop formations the dog left her, and how messy the house is...a man will listen to these things if he has to, but it isn't what he's really after.

# MAKE SPECIAL OCCASIONS

I know you don't care about this stuff as much as your wife does, but that's the point. If you're like me, you can't remember yesterday, let alone 172 events in the past and 142 still to come. I call this the too-many-penguins-on-the-iceberg theory and should patent the idea. I can fit more and more penguins on the front end of my iceberg, but the more birds I try to squeeze on, the more that fall off the back. In the same way, my head can only take on so much activity and so many people having babies every weekend. In fact, my master organ can tap out after some coffee and light reading these days.

To combat this dilemma, you have to write things down—every year, especially people who are pregnant. (It's like a bunch of hamsters out there!) If the occasion is pre-printed in your day calendar (like Christmas), all you have to do is circle it. The holidays and other reasons to celebrate sneak up on me every single year, even my own birthday. So do something different this year—plan on your lack of planning and jot it down somewhere.

Secondly, be happy about these events and quit your whining. Has your complaining ever convinced your wife that the coed bridal shower you're about to attend is really not that important? I can't tell you how many grouchy, grumpy husbands I meet every year who dread the holidays, hate going to the events their wives love, and despise even their own birthdays. Not only are they irritable, they bring everyone else down with them. Wow, what treasures to be around. Don't be like those guys. Make yourself get in the mood. (She does that for you often, I would bet.) There's an old saying that goes, "Fake it until you make it." In other words, put a big, cheesy smile on those lips until your heart catches up with your face. (You have to admit, that's a good line right there.) I like it so much I'll say it again: until your heart catches up with your face.

As of this writing, in two months my wife and I celebrate twenty-eight years (in a row) of marital bliss. Every year is not a mixture of extravagant presents, a cruise to the Caribbean, and a lobster dinner. In fact, some years it's a gift card, a paddle boat on Blue Mesa Reservoir, and Top Ramen. But the point is that I need to participate with her and think about her ahead of time, so I do. You don't want to be the guy who runs down to the Dollar Store three minutes after she hands you a gift at breakfast to try and make it right. Homer Simpson does that. Don't forget these special occasions; otherwise, you are saying she isn't special, and you didn't say a word.

# GET SOME COUNSEL

When I hear the word *counsel*, the hair on my rear end usually stands straight up. I equate it with therapy, depression, emasculation, or something far more sissy-like. I picture the dweeby guy next to a leather couch, peering over his glasses, ten or fifteen plaques on his "I love me" wall, asking me stupid questions about my marriage or, worse, my *feelings* about my marriage. Maybe I get to talk to an empty chair if I'm really lucky. (Don't laugh, I actually did that once in a session, and boy did I kick that chair's butt!)

The kind of counseling I'm talking about is different. I'm talking about seeking out a third person or couple (outsiders) for solid advice—people who are for you and for your marriage. They want it to succeed. This usually means no family members because they remember everything you ever say. Instead, I want the couple who is unbiased (if that's possible) and has "been there, done that." I want the couple who's been married forty years with lots of battle wounds to prove it. They have something worthwhile to say, a few scars, lots of wisdom, and some very practical advice. If they don't have scars that have healed from mass bleeding in the past, they don't usually have a lot to offer me.

I meet couples every now and then who say they have never argued even once. That's sweet, but I need the couple that was throwing hatchets the first few years and somehow worked it out. And they don't take sides. My wife and I were in a big fight one time about twenty-five years ago. Somehow she ended up at our mentors' house. She started down the road of telling them everything I had done wrong. (I'm sure I'd done nothing wrong as usual, but she tried to blame me anyhow.) The first question out of our mentors' mouths was, "Heidi, what did you do?" Awesome. She had done lots wrong too, and they called her on it. My kind of counselors.

It's like any topic. If you want financial advice, you seek out the guy or gal who has already made their millions. I don't talk to my poor friends who are still living paycheck to paycheck because they don't have anything for me. I also don't get a whole lot of workout counsel from the dude with a round belly. Same with marital advice. Don't go to your buddies who have been married four times or to people who have a marriage that looks like a Jerry Springer episode. Their marriage should look like what you both want, not just your "man" version of it. I have a fantasy-marriage world like you wouldn't believe, and so do you...so don't judge me!

And don't be afraid to seek advice from someone, as if you're bothering them. It actually makes me feel worthy when someone chats with me about their marital issues; shoot, I've done 99 percent of the stupid things they're trying to figure out. So don't be scared: seek out those who've gone down the road before you; someone who will tell you like it is; not necessarily a friend, but someone twenty years your senior who has worked through lots of crap.

Just the other day we had a lady say she didn't want to put her husband down in front of other people, so she didn't seek outside counsel. Sounds right, but here are my thoughts on that one: Don't seek counsel to talk about your spouse. Seek counsel to talk about *you*, because you need to fix you first. Believe me, you weren't raised right either, and you have some jacked-up thinking about what this marriage thing looks like as well. So man up and go get some counsel (I mean therapy). Do you have any idea what it's like being married to you?

# TAKE THE LEAD

A man may let his woman pick the church they go to, if he goes at all, because he loves her. This sounds sweet and humble on the front end, but think about it for a moment. If your wife picks out the church and you follow her lead, the chances of you still going a year later are slim, especially if you don't care too much for "churchy" things. The preaching has no bearing on your life, the worship time gives you a chance to get a catnap because the music kind of blows, and they are always asking for your money. Wow, sign me up! What normal man would do this when faced with a good football game instead? (By the way, go Broncos!) Every Sunday you are faced with the dilemma of how to get out of it, so you come up with projects like desperately needing to clean the garage, possibly organizing your tools, or a sudden desire to pet the cat. (Never mind, all cats are doomed anyhow.)

Now change it up for a second. Let's say you man up because you and your family are in crisis (again), and *you* decide to take your family to church. Go find one that speaks the truth. If they are always flapping about hell, go somewhere else. If they never talk about hell (or the cats that go with it), go somewhere else. If they never preach on money, something's wrong. If they always preach on money, don't give them any. If they insist on drinking the Kool-Aid, you know what to do. If the music still sucks after a year, learn to play an instrument. The point is to go to a church that really turns your crank. I only go where the preaching is good, the worship is good, the kids love it, and I can walk away glad that I went. Go to a church you actually like, and 99 percent of the time your family will follow you. That's a big part of being a man. You have to take the lead, though.

Not that your spouse shouldn't be active in all the things I just mentioned, but it is *your* responsibility to make sure these things happen. Maybe you're not that spiritual of a person. So what are you waiting for? Get spiritual. You already have a spirit, now feed it. When I first got married, my wife and I were not quite so spiritual. She used to bribe me with sex every Sunday about 9:00 a.m., the time we would normally leave for church. Guess what? For a twenty-year-old, it worked. I quit going to church. Unfortunately for her, I became more and more of a J-E-R-K (my Myers-Briggs personality indicator at the time). She even told a friend of ours back then, "Do you have any studies or something my husband can do? He was a lot nicer when he was doing that church thing." Now that I am older and wiser, I can see through all this (not that she bribes me any longer). The point is this: it is my job to make sure my wife and family stay on track. We've been going to church for twenty-six years now, and guess what? We are all a lot nicer. We are more alive than ever. And it takes a lot more than sex to keep me home on Sunday (a sure sign of spiritual maturity...or old age).

There are other spiritual things besides church too. How about a good marriage study or evening devotions with the kids before bed? When was the last time you suggested praying with your wife? (Did you just throw up in your mouth a little? Good; I'm on the right path.) Surround yourself with people who encourage you and lift you and your family up. Don't care for hypocrites? Me either. (We're all hypocrites, by the way; it's just that real men go to church to do something about it.) So find people who walk the talk and hang around them often. We all have souls that need to be nourished, just like our bodies. If it is my job to put food on the table, it is also my job to get the souls of my family fed. And this isn't just to check a block off my to-do list. This is what taking care of your spouse and your children really looks like. Who cares how alive your pocketbook is if your soul hasn't been fed in five years. Some of you men truly are *The Walking Dead*. Wake up. Take the spiritual lead. Drag your family with you if you have to.

# LOVE YOUR CHILDREN

For most of us, this isn't a difficult thing. We have different renditions of love, of course, but most of us love our children automatically. I used to come home after a fun-filled day in the army and roll around on the floor with my kids for at least an hour. It wasn't a chore either—I liked it. My wife, however, was tortured because of all the noise. Fortunately, we have wood floors these days...so the scream acoustics are even better! There's nowhere else to go (and no army these days), so we pile up somewhere between the kitchen and the living room. In fact, we don't even use the term *pile*, we say "pie hole." If we both plan to crush the third person, it's called an "(insert their name) sandwich." That's love in our house. Try it...even if they are twenty-two.

I do have a friend, however, who struggled with loving his kids. He loved them in his own way, but not the way he should have because he was very neglected growing up. He had no idea how he was coming across. So one day, after I got to know him a little better, I told him something like, "This is going to sting a little, so let me know when you are ready." He said, "Go for it; I know you love me." So I said, "You treat your kids like dogs." And he did. He took their ice-cream cones and threw them away once because they didn't eat them fast enough. With that one, I said, "Why don't you let them enjoy their lives?" Apparently I was the first person to tell him these things, but a lot of people had felt this way after watching him over the years. Luckily, he was one of those guys who took things to heart and was very teachable when someone confronted him on his crap. I noticed an immediate change in him as a father. He didn't fix everything overnight, but it was and still is on his mind constantly after that, and I admire him for it. It's a good thing too, because he and his wife are still popping them little babies out like a self-run chinchilla farm.

So do you really love your kids? Do you have "pie holes" with them after work? Are they a burden to you or a joy when you walk in the door? Do you enjoy helping them with their homework, or would you prefer to watch television or just write all day? You only have one shot to get it right… and by the way, you probably won't get it right. But the point is not to waste your time during the child-rearing phase of life. This is your time, and more importantly, it's your children's time. This is their childhood, and they only get one, so make it rock. Make it enjoyable and challenging. Work hard and play hard—together—all the time. Mold them.

Take them with you whenever you can. There is something to learn every single day. That's love. In addition, you get an awesome opportunity to create a "mini me," or a "mini you" in this case.

Take my fourteen-year-old, for example. He is the epitome of sarcasm because of me. Most of it is quite funny, but some of it, I wonder what I've already done for and to his future spouse. We have a bad habit in our home, and it's all my fault. I thought it was funny that every time I had to sneeze, I wouldn't necessarily cover my face...at all. I would pretty much just aim for the backs of the kids' shirts, just to watch them flap in the breeze. I don't know how your sneezes come out, but I can give my kids a new part on the scalp from seven yards out if I were to aim it right, so I go for the shirt back.

This brings me to one evening not that long ago. My son, Cruz, decided it was his turn to sneeze on Dad. No problem with his theory of getting back at me...his problem was that he blasted the side of my face with some snot shrapnel at 212 mph from about three inches of my right eye hole. I felt it immediately. After the beatings of retaliation and another teaching moment, we had a good laugh about it. (Just kidding...we never laughed about it.) Love on those kids, my brothers.

# GIVE QUANTITY TIME

This has nothing to do with the title, but it's worth noting: I said sarcastically (surprise) to my wife last night after a few funny jabs at each other, "Better to live on the corner of the roof than with a nagging wife, and Heidi said, "Better for me to live on the corner of the roof if you aren't going to follow through with what you said." (Please send all rebuttals directly to my wife as I don't have one yet.)

OK, back on topic while women around the world cheer. Some men take this idea and rationalize their contributions to the family, particularly the workaholics out there—and you know who you are. Often, we men think as long as the tiny bit of time we do spend with our wives is quality time, we are doing really well. I have even heard friends of mine say things like, "I don't get to spend a lot of time with the family, but when I do, I am totally locked on." Not so fast, my young Padawan.

Let's say I have you over for dinner and feed you the most delicious, incredible-tasting lobster you have ever had. (This will never happen, but let's say I did.) The only problem is that I decide to load you up with a whopping two ounces and the dinner is over. Would you be satisfied? No. Same with our wives and families. Quality time is only beneficial if it comes in decent enough quantity at the same time. Both have to be in sync with each other to be of any value. They need to see your fat face every day if possible, and you need to be there to tuck them in as often as you can. Wives need tucking too. (Hey, wait a minute, what a great bumper sticker that would make: Have you tucked your wife today?)

Secondly, quantity time has to have some quality to it. You can't be watching a football game four days a week and having quality anything…except maybe quality yelling when one of the kids is blocking the TV. And don't try going to the movies for quality time, as I mentioned before—this doesn't count. Quality time is interacting with each other, face to face, heart to heart, with meaningful conversation. In fact, one of the key questions for my fourteen-year-old is, "What are you doing with your life?" And then I usually tell him he only has until Friday to figure it out. That sparks conversation and a wrestling match every time.

There are days when I'm just not in the mood for quality or quantity. This is sometimes OK (unless you feel this way every day). My wife and I will finally get back to the house some days, and I'll say something awesome like, "I just want to be a slug tonight." Translation: My mental capacity was extinguished somewhere else. She's usually OK with this until I develop a five-day pattern of it. Other times, we've gone to dinner and I didn't even look up at her for the first twenty minutes. I was so mesmerized by the steak and potatoes on my plate, with elbows and forks flying, I didn't look up until there was just leftover A.1. Sauce and a few bacon bits scattered about. (That's actually somewhat of a lie...I would never leave bacon bits.) This isn't quality time, even though we were out to dinner, and it wasn't quantity because I wolfed my food in thirty seconds—thank you, US military, for that fine habit ingrained in me for life.

Other times we have just taken a walk for some window-shopping and had pretty deep conversations or gone on a long drive when we didn't intend on it. So try to be purposeful, get out of the flipping house, get off the corner of the roof for dang sure, and make her life fuller. Then you'll be allowed to give her quantity time at 2:00 a.m. to boot. I mean quality.

# LEARN TO SERVE

Of all the spiritual gifts out there, this is one I don't have. I like and acknowledge the *idea* of serving, but not actually *doing* the serving. Serving blows. Realizing the need to serve is one thing; acting on it is another. I do serve my wife, however, and you need to serve yours. This can take a variety of forms, obviously (and thankfully). I keep offering to serve my wife in sexual ways, but she never seems to take me up on it.

For example, my wife loves to have the bed made...every single day. This makes no sense to me. I'm going to climb right back in it at night and mess it up again. That's like washing dishes before you put them in the dishwasher and wiping before you poop. Sorry to be so crass, but word pictures are important. Sometimes she is so eager to make the bed, I'm still in it. Her preference is that I jump out and make it with her and then get dressed for the day. This is completely alien to how a man thinks. I don't mind grabbing a corner and doing "the big tsunami" with the comforter, but then I'm out. Oh no. She likes everything neatly tucked with only a couple of our thirty-two pillows facing certain directions, color coordinated, seams to one side, allowance for ambience, bigger pillows neatly placed in a "cuddle pile" to help with global warming (I think). Apparently, our cat has its own pillow as well. But to her, that's how she wants to be served, so I do my best to participate regardless of what I think. Don't get me started on the cat, though.

On a similar note, I have a friend who has always been excellent with cars. He loves to keep them in top working order, even better than when you may have lent it to him. While his wife appreciated his auto skills over the years, what she wanted was help around the house and more help raising their four kids. He never did those other things too well, however, and they are no longer married. I can't say his tinkering in the garage was singularly to blame, but it certainly had its influence because he always served his wife in ways *he* thought was best. He bent over backward doing things *he* thought were important and a good role for the husband to perform. In his mind, everything else was women's work. Now he does the man's work and the woman's work (whatever that is) because he is all by himself. Don't be that guy. Sincerity isn't enough. Figure out ways to serve that actually minister to your wife in a way where she feels the love. Don't bust your butt in the garage when she really wants you to change a diaper. Don't be phenomenal at detailing the car if what she really needs is someone to help her clean dog poop off the carpet. Don't keep the yard immaculate if she would prefer help in the kitchen. I'm not saying to neglect the former things; I'm saying to put your energy into the things where you get the biggest bang for the buck. Serve smarter, not harder, and never confuse your busyness with real accomplishment.

# LEARN TO TOUCH

Most of us men are thinking, "Trust me, I have learned to touch." Stick with me for a minute there, Rambo. Most women love hugs and kisses, but not all. The kind of touch I'm talking about comes down to knowing what your wife likes. I didn't say what *you* think she likes—I said what *she* actually likes. Some women have been touched inappropriately over the years, and so physical touch is more of a sensitive issue with them to begin with. You have to be very careful here. Other women want you to hug them, hold hands, kiss them in public, and have constant contact in some form 24-7. And I implore you: if your wife needs more touch from you, give it to her without question.

I used to grab my wife's rear end constantly. It wasn't that I was trying to be disrespectful or rude—I honestly thought it was cute, and so I always grabbed it, maybe just to give it some encouragement here and there. The problem was that my wife didn't like it. I would defend myself and tell her all the reasons why I needed to squeeze it...for her benefit. What really made it bad was that I did it in public as well. I wasn't trying to embarrass her, either—I just took it upon myself to lift her spirits at home, in the car, standing in line, swimming, wherever necessary. Sounds kind of silly now that I'm putting it in writing, but at the time I was really thinking it was a good thing and that she needed to see it for what I was really trying to accomplish. (See how the emphasis was on me, not on her. Epic fail.) The part I missed was that she hated it for about fifteen years or so before I got a clue. I learned over the years that she likes soft touches and only in nonsexual places like a hand, an eyebrow, or possibly an earlobe.

Now for most of us men, this ruins our philosophy as to why we got married in the first place. The whole idea is for a man to grope his wife at will due to the ring he put on her finger. This too is all made up in our heads regarding what marriage should look like. Unfortunately, if you want to have a good marriage, you can't fondle your wife at will, as much as you would like to. Some of you may have a wife who lets you do this. If you are one of those men, I don't want to hear from you, ever, because you don't live in the real world with the rest of us.

That reminds me of another form of touching I used to do that she also hated. For some reason (maybe raging hormones or the fact I was in my twenties and so full of wisdom), I used to think it was OK to lean on her—wait for it—pelvis out. And I mean way out, almost with an arched back. Maybe it was a subtle form of ownership, like I was proving to the world that my wife and I had sexual contact as often as needed during our off-hours and this was just a small sample of what our homelife was really like. Funny now, but dumb. (I still stand that way now, but my belly hits everything first these days, so there's nothing sexual about it.)

The big concept here is to figure out your woman's style of touch. If she doesn't have one, you'll have to help her develop one. In some rare cases, the man is the one who doesn't like to be touched. I can't fathom that as easily, but if you're that guy, make sure you go out of your way to touch your woman often, even if you have to force yourself. Eventually it will become a habit. Be it hugs or caressing her hair or whatever she likes, you both need to develop a proper habit of touching the right way at the right time where you both win. And here's an idea we men rarely think of: ask her. Ask her what she likes and dislikes and then (unlike me for all those years) respond accordingly. If there's one thing I have learned, it's this: when your wife genuinely says she doesn't like the way you touch her, not one time will you catch her lying.

# BUY *HER* FLOWERS

I don't care how rough and gruff your woman is (even if she has a small moustache and a voice deeper than yours), every woman likes flowers. I know it's pointless—that's the point. Flowers are nothing more than weeds in bloom to us men, but our women love them. I'm not sure why ladies love flowers the way they do—maybe it's because the flowers are soon going to die and they cost way too much for the short-term gain. It's a mercy purchase for me, really. Maybe wives know we'll be forced to buy them again soon, and therefore because of the meaningless nature of flowers and the fact they keep you thinking of her, flowers have even more value to her than other purchases.

For whatever reason, flowers get you decent bang for the buck. You don't have to do anything but buy something she likes. Even the crappy flowers will get you a smile because you did it for her, especially if you do it for no special occasion. This also works if you aren't a flower-buying guy yet and this will be your first colored-weed purchase ever. (On a side note due to my plethora of experiences, do *not* buy pink flowers around Christmastime. I did this exact thing one year, and they did not receive a warm welcome because they were not color coordinated for the season.) That being said, you can't do a fifty-meter sprint through Safeway and grab the first low-hanging fruit of flower carnage dangling near the register; you have to take at least sixty seconds of real thought and get *her* type of flowers. So you need to find out which flowers are in fact going to do more good than harm. You probably didn't know this was even possible until just now, so you are welcome. Let me illustrate.

My wife says mums and daisies are not "real" flowers. Wow, apparently I'm not smarter than a fifth grader or the produce lady. Oh, and guess what all stores within the nearest seventy-five-mile radius of my house sell the most of? I tried a Venus flytrap once, thinking I was going to up the ante and buy my bride a whole plant that would live for years—a constant (yet annual) reminder of my devotion and love. What's cooler than a flower that also eats meat? She wasn't as impressed as my teenage son was.

No, she likes the most expensive flowers that only grow during high tide, twenty-five-year blood moons, in one specific oasis region of the Gobi Desert, behind a waterfall, in March, during leap year. I still cannot pronounce the flower. All I know is that it looks like a purple star with some acne and has a little squad of clone troopers in attack formation bursting out of its pie hole. It's actually a stargazer lily, but only florists in New Delhi carry it…that part is true, sort of.

They're harder to find than lost airliners in the ocean. She loves these things, though, so guess what I look for when I'm in the Indian section of Safeway? But don't just buy your wife flowers to check it off your list. Buy *her* flowers.

# DON'T INTERRUPT HER

I did this very thing this morning. Fail. I was reading and minding my own business. The emphasis is on "minding my own business" as if I am all that matters prior to having coffee, which is partially true. My bride came in and kissed me on the cheek (because I had some serious morning-chewed-on-pillow-leftover-steak-coffee breath). She started off by saying, "I have some thoughts…" Blah, blah, blah… my mind went elsewhere. I thought she was going to start talking about these cabins we bought last year and are still trying to renovate. I get sick of the cabin conversation and their related business discussions some days, and this morning was one of them. So being as loving and patient as I so often am, I interrupted her and said, "Can I just have fifteen minutes of downtime before we start talking business?" That went over like a fart in church. So much for my kiss on the cheek; I'd just ruined the morning with thirteen words in less than ten seconds. Turns out after my twelve-minute apology, seventeen minutes of convincing her I did in fact want to hear her thoughts, and one more cup of joe that she was just sharing something deep in her heart. In my infinite ability to read her mind (and you thought only women could do this), I'd stomped on her ideas and her soul before I'd heard a word. Nice Saturday, Rob.

You may not think you do this very often, but you're probably guiltier than you think if you're breathing in and out. People in general do this a lot more often than what we should. Added to that is the fact that if you're male, you think your opinion is not only more valid, but more important than anything she could be saying at any given moment. If you don't believe me, ask her if you are an inter-rupter. I dare you! If she says no, you may skip this section and go to the next one. Even Scripture says that a fool finds no pleasure in understanding but delights in airing his own opinions. If this is you, God says you are a fool. Did I mention how foolish this is yet? Let her talk. Let your mind go blank for a minute. (For some, this is no problem.) Let her finish her thoughts. And then don't just spout off your reply filled with your supposed nuggets of wisdom, but repeat what she just said to you and ask her if you really got it. Now *this* is real conversation.

I can't tell you how many times I have jumped in head-first (or gotten mad for that matter), because I thought she was going to say something else—about my bad eating habits, how to better love others, or my favorite, how not to ridicule the other idiots on the highway. Instead of talking about the issue, now we get to instead argue over my inter-ruption for an extra ten minutes or how I "always" interrupt and "never" let her talk. The Bible says, "He who answers before listening; that is his folly and his shame" (Prov. 18:13). It says "his shame," so God must be talking about you. Don't interrupt, my brothers. Don't be a fool. Don't answer before listening. Don't force yourself to do the walk of shame on a fine Saturday morning.

# OPEN HER DOOR

O K, manly men, this is another easy one for which you will get lots of credit...and it's free! Opening a door for your spouse is an expression of love. Many couples will say they are no longer in love or simply fell out of love. You cannot fall out of love—an airplane maybe or possibly a roller coaster, but not love. In the words of Hans and Franz, "Hear me now, listen to me later." Falling out of love is not possible. The only thing that's possible is that one or both of you chose to stop doing the loving things you used to do. Remember, love is an action—something you are or are not supposed to do.

For example, I asked in a marriage study one night, "What's the most irritating habit your husband still engages in that you wish he wouldn't?" I expected 99 percent of the wives to complain about their gassy husbands. One wife, however, commented that she wished her husband would quit biting his toenails and spitting them in the sink. You heard it correctly: I said "biting," "toenails," and "spitting" in the same sentence. So in his case, it would also be loving not to put his big cheesy toes in his mouth and then expect romantic, sloppy kisses later. You have your own nonloving issues, I'm sure.

If I open the car door for my wife, I am loving her right that moment. If I ever stop, I am no longer loving her in that area of her life. Sometimes, after fifty years (or five minutes) go by, we stop doing the things we did while we were dating. Don't be that guy. Always open the door to the house and to the car and to elevators and banks and grocery stores, no matter how irritated you are, even if you are in a fight, no matter what she is saying about you, no matter the weather, and especially no matter what the feminazis are chanting. Love shouldn't ever stop, and it isn't based on your feelings. If it were, you would rarely do anything. I guarantee she will love it if you do this one thing (although there are thousands more). So don't stop opening her doors...ever.

# DO CULTURAL STUFF

I'm pretty sure this is a verse in the Bible, in the back, near the maps. Don't go to this cultural stuff because you like it, but because *she* does. I know there are some dudes who actually like this stuff...and that's why we can only be friends on Facebook.

The other day, my bride and I went to a show in Denver that involved horses and acrobatics...on purpose. (You know how it says in Scripture that a thousand years is like a day to the Lord? In my case, I use the phrase, "the other day," which can be yesterday or twelve years ago.) It was her birthday, so aside from doing it to be the loving husband I am, I was twice as obligated. Oh, and by the way, my wife doesn't celebrate just one day; she celebrates what she calls her "birthday month." This means I'm supposed to love her even more each day and exceed all expectations for thirty days straight. (You might want to hide this paragraph.)

So there I was, ten days before her actual birthday, setting up reservations to go to a famous donkey show (I mean horse-acrobatic-triple-flip-half-gainer extravaganza). Now I don't dislike horses, but they don't really turn my crank either. In fact, a lovely 1500-pound horse stood on my chest once as a child during a vacation to Arkansas (thanks for having relatives there, oh father of mine). So I never went on a horse-riding spree after that incident, but I don't really give a rip about horses is what I mean. But I thought, "Who knows, maybe the show will be worth it." And when I say, "worth it," I mean good bang for the buck. I can pay fifty dollars for a good steak and not feel cheated, but if I pay $1.25 for a bark-seaweed-lawnmower-shaving sandwich, I'll want $13.50 in change.

It wasn't worth it, at least not for what I paid. The cheap tickets were seventy dollars each, but there was print in a 0.2-point font at the bottom that read these seats came with a "partially obstructed view." (The last time I had a "partially obstructed view" was on a cruise ship where there was a full-size smokestack salvaged from the Titanic outside our porthole window. The trip wasn't a total waste, however, as my family has since coined the phrase "shut your porthole.") So I paid for the one hundred dollar seats to please my wife—not the most expensive, but not the cheapest ones either. Sadly, I still had an obstructed view due to the six-foot-five Amazon woman who sat in front of me. Then there was the actual show.

It wasn't bad, just not two hundred dollars' worth of entertainment. (I can go snowboarding all day with the whole family for that price...with lunches.) I think I got a solid twelve dollars' worth of entertainment. Oh, and I had to pay another fifteen dollars to the asphalt Nazis so I could park because pavement in Denver is never free. At the end of the day, my wife said she absolutely loved it. I debated as to whether I should have responded, but I have learned over the years, so I said nothing, kept my porthole shut, and it remains a fond memory in her mind.

Our wives love this stuff. Don't try to understand it. Don't try to wonder if you are getting a good bang for your buck because most of the time you probably aren't—at least not in terms of the event. It is absolutely worth the dividends it pays in terms of your relationship, however. I can't wait to pay three hundred dollars to go see an opera that makes no sense this fall…she's worth it.

# HOUSE NOTES
# EVERYWHERE

This one sounds a little girly, but it pays big dividends. (It's even better than a card because you get to write notes from your own twisted heart.) Again, it doesn't cost much, it's easy to do (provided you can write without it looking like it was done with a crayon in your left hand), and it demonstrates that you actually give a poop. I know you think working sixty to eighty hours a week is a clear demonstration that you do care—not so, my workaholic. That's what I'm trying to tell you…your little note will tell her more than your entire week at work does, and it doesn't take more than one minute (in a row).

One time I got really clever. I took one of my wife's lipsticks and wrote a very loving note on the mirror, certain she would see it before she headed out the door. The words were perfect. The idea was brilliant. The encouragement was needed, and she certainly did see it. Apparently, I used her favorite lipstick, however. Don't do this, my brothers. Find the lime-green color she never uses. (If you married an emo-goth-filed-teeth-tattoo-pierced-eyebrow-chain-tied-to-lips-type lady, no telling what color lipstick you need to use. Try blood, I guess.)

And don't get stuck on my one idea. Put notes next to the coffeepot. Put one in her Punky Brewster lunch box if she still has one, or even under her pillow. Shoot, you could even tape one to the dog's rear end for that matter. At least she would see it the next time he's scooting across your white carpet leaving you a souvenir.

You could send her on a treasure hunt using notes too, where one note leads to the next. I did this for her birthday one year, and she enjoyed the hunt. I was taking her to the island of Saipan for her birthday. (Don't think I'm rich or spoiled; we lived on the island of Guam, about a thirty-minute flight away.) I took a psychology book and covered up the part that said "ology," leaving the "psych" portion exposed. Then I took a frying pan and hid it in another location. Her clues were the book and the pan to piece together. She didn't figure it out, but she still talks about the effort I went through all these years later. Oh yeah, score number 197 for the Glegster! Leave her a note or two. It's like the common wheel; it works every time it's tried.

# TIME FOR RECREATION

*R*ecreation literally means "to re-create; to make fresh again; to make new." Some of you haven't recreated in fifteen years. (I didn't say procreated.) You aren't new, you aren't fresh, and your life is frankly starting to stink. If you're one of those guys who never takes time off work, you need to rethink your priorities (and read the last section about getting your priorities straight). We all need downtime; even God says to fully rest at least one day a week. If you don't take a break, and I mean often, you aren't that fun to be around anyhow. Ever meet those people who never stop? I mean they don't stop! I'm not saying there's no place for hard work, but you have to stop doing stuff more frequently than you think.

Now, let me add another cog to the wheel before you decide to take up golfing all by yourself. Not only do you need to take a break, you need to find some activities that you can do with your wife. This part is hard. My wife loves artsy-fartsy kind of things. She could hang out in Hobby Lobby for a week. (I would put something sharp in my eye if I had to do that.) She loves to shop and spend money and "look" at clothes for hours. (I can't say I love shopping at all unless I have a specific target in mind—like a fishing pole or a camping stove.) She loves live music and dancing and all the things that give her life more zest. (I like to sit back with a cup of coffee and watch people that have the zest.) She thinks it's fun to hike...uphill. (That's not recreation, that's prep for an Iron Man.) The key is to find something you both like to do or something the whole family can do together if you have little mini yous.

My wife and I took a quiz once that listed hundreds of activities. We were supposed to independently circle every event we thought we would enjoy to rejuvenate our souls. When we finished and compared notes, we had exactly two activities that we'd both circled that fit criteria for the whole family—camping and skiing. So from that moment on, we decided that we would be a camping family for six months and a ski/snowboard family for the other six. (Of course I convinced the kids that they also liked fishing and hot chocolate as part of their downtime.)

In any case, we go camping at least once a month from May to October and hit the slopes November through April. My wife paints on canvas near the rivers while the rest of us fish and splash water on each other. Other times, after a weekend of ski/snowboard/lip skidding down the mountain, we hit the hot springs on the way back and have full-on WWE water-wrestling matches among the other tourists trying to relax. Sometimes we camp for a week at a pop, but I noticed if we do that, my wife needs a break from the woods to rejuvenate from her rejuvenation...and a serious bath. We even camped at the ski slopes once—I do not recommend pulling a travel trailer through the Sierra Nevadas in winter...ever.

Have you ever met one of those families who makes you feel guilty because they serve at the homeless shelter every Saturday, run marathons in their spare time, learn a foreign language together on Wednesdays, and then go on a mission trip to Mexico every three months while you go camping? I have. I don't make comparisons anymore; we do what our family has decided we need to do for our sanity. This doesn't mean we don't serve or reach out to others. We do. Shoot, we did it last night. But if I need to recreate, it won't involve running in any form.

# YOUR STRAIGHT
# PRIORITIES

Warning: PG-13 ahead I (as if it hasn't been all along. You know how to tell when you're getting older than you thought? When your wife says, "Do you want a quickie?" and you respond with, "No, I want a coffee!" Yes, that actually happened. Man, are my priorities jacked up sometimes! Now it's midday, and I wish I had taken her up on this rare offer.

I was reading my favorite Bible book (Ecclesiastes) this morning after five whole hours of sleep. I like it because it basically says to pull your head out and live right, keeping your priorities in order. So simple, but so tough to carry out. The subheading read "Solomon's Downfall." Solomon basically said (for the twenty-sixth time for me), that he had all the money, all the power of a king, and all the women he wanted. He "denied himself no pleasure and had every-thing a man could desire." (I realize, on paper, that money is not the answer, but I would like to try it once and test my theory.) He goes on to state that there is nothing bet-ter than to enjoy food (no problem there) and drink and to find satisfaction in your work—these pleasures are from the hand of God. "Talk is cheap. Fear God instead" (Eccles. 5:7). "Those who love money will never have enough" (Eccles. 5:10). The more you have, the more people come to help you spend it. Enjoy what you have rather than desir-ing what you don't have. "Finishing is better than starting" (Eccles. 7:8). "The wife God gives you is your reward for all your earthly toil" (Eccles. 9:9). Wow!

If you don't have time to talk to and enjoy your "God-given wife in reward for your toil," your priorities are messed up. Your life is not about your work, although you have sev-eral jobs to do and you are supposed to do them well. Your life is not about your hobbies either. You can hunt, fish, and play golf all you want, but those things shouldn't be what you are known for. Your life should mostly be about God, your wife, and the kids because guess what? You and I are going to die someday. Say it with me: d-i-e. That means to no longer live; to quit breathing; snuffed out; your time in the spotlight is over; dead; running with the angels; over; caput.

Not that long ago, I had a doctor tell me he found two spots on my lungs during an x-ray. He said if it was lung cancer, there was nothing he could do about it. He then told me to go home and come back in three months and he would check again. I went home that day with several thoughts on my mind: Did I live my life well? Why go to work anymore? No need to wash the car...ever. TV isn't that important after all. Did I spend enough time with my wife and children, or was I going to have to scramble and make up for lost time? Had I made the right decisions over the years regarding my military career? What would I change if given the chance to do it over? Do I need to shave the cat?

I can honestly say that I felt really good about the amount of time I had spent with my family. I had made decisions that actually hurt my career but paid big dividends with my family. It was then I realized I wouldn't change anything in that area of my life: I had done the right things for the most part—at least the things that mattered. God was number one, and should be...this is eternity we're talking about. You might want to consider checking Him out. What good is it to gain the whole world and forfeit your soul? My family was number two—maybe fifty years of your life, if you are lucky. My career was number three—twenty-eight years I put forth and now it rarely crosses my mind as to what I used to do for a living (except for the push-ups in the snow). My priorities were straight and still are, especially now because I don't have a career any longer...nor do I miss it. The money was good, but the freedom is better.

I was ready to die. I didn't need a do-over with God or my family. Another career maybe, but that's still up for debate. We all make mistakes, but we must learn to fail small. For some of you reading this, you need to make adjustments starting today. For you other dudes, you just got confirmation that you are doing exactly what you need to be doing, so keep plugging along.

Incidentally, I went back to the doctor three months later and he said, "I don't know what happened, but the spots are gone." I didn't know whether to be excited or punch him in the face for leaving food on the microfilm. I never found out what happened, but I can tell you that I continue living for what matters most. Put a sign on the fridge if you have to (since you frequent that location most), but keep your life in the right order. Finishing is better than how you start. Finishing well is the best. That's how you will be remembered anyhow.

# NOT THE END

The heading above is self-explanatory—it means to move on and keep doing what we need to do. But since you are already on the last couple pages, let me say this: this is not a self-help book. This isn't about you; it's about her. Marriage is not a fifty-fifty relationship like you hear at the theaters. It is one hundred-one hundred all the time, all day, every day. This means you do everything you can 100 percent of the time and don't worry about her keeping up on her end. If you're disappointed I haven't said anything to women, guess what? I wasn't speaking to women. This was for you men. If I were writing to women (and I will someday), I would have plenty to say to them. But this is your time. This is your opportunity on stage, so don't waste it. It's not how long you have dated or how old you are. It's really about if you're ready to work at one of the most important things you can do on this Earth. Your days are numbered, so live them right, all the time. You will only harvest what you plant; maybe your marriage is suffering because you aren't throwing out any seed, yet you're standing there waiting for a crop to magically produce itself.

Where does all the love go after the wedding? I'm glad you asked. Love is an act of will. Always has been. Love is an action, not a feeling. We fall into a pit maybe, but we do not fall in love, and we don't fall out of it either. Let's face it—we marry for the dumbest reasons. Some women get married because they like the idea of being loved by another man so much they sweat little heart-shaped spores. Men are simpler, like I said at the beginning. We marry because "she's kind of cute" or maybe "she was kind of pregnant." Doesn't really matter.

You know what prompted me to pop the question to my seventeen-year-old girlfriend all those years back? I got stuck in the sand with my way-cool four-wheel-drive pickup truck. Little miss hot mess was sitting on her side of the truck doing her nails, while I was on the outside digging with my hands to set us free. Out pops my Barbie-like chicklet, and she starts digging on her side of the truck. "That's the woman for me," I thought. I asked her to marry me that same evening. What basis was this for marriage? I'll tell you: none. It isn't how you start that matters, no matter how jacked up your reasoning for getting married. What matters is how you finish. It's not the first day of your marriage you should evaluate, but the last day of your marriage that counts.

This is why I came up with the list. This will blow away any honey-do scratch pad she will ever give you, so keep this manual in a safe place and read it often. Besides, lists make us think, and we need to spend our time not just doing things, but doing the most important things. Being busy all the time doesn't mean you're being productive. If you actually do the things I've laid out for you, you'll be choosing to really love her and will therefore actually be in love. Again, love is not a gaseous feeling somewhere in your gut, but a "doing" with your heart and your hands. These things are simple. I said they're simple; I did not say they're going to be easy to carry out. One last thing: when you feel you're at the end of your marital rope, tie a knot and keep holding on because marriage is the number one cause for divorce today. You got this.

# ABOUT THE AUTHOR

Rob Gleghorn is first and foremost a man of God (or at least that's his goal), a husband of just one wife (that he knows of) a father of two children (currently fifteen and eleven), a church leader, a self-proclaimed comedian (just ask him), a teacher, a business owner, and a Gulf War and Iraq War veteran. Having served in both the US Air Force and the US Army, enlisted and as an officer, he finally retired at the rank of major in 2013. He has written one book—this one. However, an in-depth book with more humor and real-life war stories on how to get a life is now in the making after five years of research and extensive plagiarizing of God's word. Rob has a bachelor of arts in history and education from Western State Colorado University, a master of science in international relations from Troy University, and a master of arts in national security studies from the American Military

University. Most importantly, he will tell you that the Holy Spirit, his unique sense of humor, reading the Bible twenty-nine times, memorizing over eight hundred Scriptures, and being married to his beautiful bride (without any breaks) for the last twenty-eight years have given him more education, training, and character development than all his other experiences and education combined.

Made in the USA
San Bernardino, CA
11 April 2017